D1553239

Beyond the Beyond
My Journey to Destiny

by

Paul "Doc" Gaccione

Brighton Publishing LLC
501 W. Ray Road
Suite 4
Chandler, AZ 85225
www.BrightonPublishing.com

Beyond the Beyond
My Journey to Destiny

by

Paul "Doc" Gaccione

Brighton Publishing LLC
501 W. Ray Road
Suite 4
Chandler, AZ 85225
www.BrightonPublishing.com

First Edition

Printed in the United States of America
Copyright © 2011

ISBN 13: 978-1-936587-52-0
ISBN 10: 1-936-58752-1

Cover Design by Tom Rodriquez

ᏔAcknowledgements Ꮛ

First and foremost, I would like to give honor and my humbling and deepest gratitude to God the Almighty and His Living and Holy Spirit. Without God, I would have not been able to complete my story of *Beyond the Beyond.*

To my mom and dad's spirits, for which I was driven to tell this story. I acknowledge my four children: Paul, Gina, Marcus, and Brian, who, through hard times, have always given me their unconditional love. They have always given me inspiration. I also give thanks to all my children's spouses for their support.

I acknowledge the three loves that I have had in my lifetime: Louise, Angie and Marie. The love I have for them will always remain in my heart. To my nephew, John, with whom I've always had a special closeness. I acknowledge the love I have for my two brothers: John and Mark. My special thanks to my entire family and friends who have made it possible for me to be free from my incarceration and to be let out on bail.

A special thanks I give to my friend, Ron Kist, who led the way for so many of my friends to come to my need. To just mention a few: Johnny Liuzzi, Tommy and Anthony

1

Ciardella, Bobby Gireffa, Richie Pezzolla, George Pepe, and Louise Lembo Kuhnle.

I would like to make a special acknowledgment to my son, Brian; my daughter, Gina; and my girlfriend, Marie; for their tireless efforts to make it possible for me to fulfill my destiny. A special thanks and gratitude to my sister-in-law, Donna Marie, for the endless time she has put into the work of this book. Finally, I would like to acknowledge Dinesh D'Souza for his contribution by the writing of his book, *Life After Death: The Evidence,* and for his God-given intellect. This book gave me the courage to go forth with telling my story of *Beyond the Beyond.* I give thanks and gratitude that destiny has put this man in my path.

Surely God would not have created such a being as man, with an ability to grasp the infinite, to exist only for a day! No, no, man was made for immortality. —Abraham Lincoln

‹ꙮ *Forward* ꙮ›

I guess I am considered a high profile person being that the FBI and the New York Organized Crime Task Force claim that I am a member of the Mafia. I was indicted and arrested in April of 2010 for murder. I spent six months in Rikers Island Jail before being released on $1,000,000.00 bail.

About two years ago, I was inspired to write a manuscript telling of some incredible spiritual experiences which had occurred in my life. I have been given the courage to write my story by Dinesh D'Souza, the author of *Life After Death: The Evidence*. How ironic that I have been inspired to write a manuscript, since I have no literary skills and have never read a book.

I start my writing by telling my life story—telling about all the near misses I have had with fame and fortune. My main purpose is to give you the opportunity to determine for yourself my credibility as I tell the story of my journey to the *Beyond the Beyond*. The other purpose is to show how many hats I have worn in my life and how many different experiences I have had in life—also, to show how many signs I had received throughout my life before I was able to see my purpose in life, and to know what road my destiny was on.

௸ *Introduction* ௸

As far back as I can remember, despite me being a scrawny kid who could barely see, my dream and aspiration was to become the heavyweight champion of the world. Maybe it was because my father had me watch boxing matches on TV since I was a little boy.

As life passed by, those dreams were not to be. I always felt that I had a special calling in life.

Throughout my life, and from time to time, I would see some signs—so I always kept one eye open waiting for my calling.

Well! It has arrived in the story of the *Beyond the Beyond.*

This is the story of my crazy life—a life that has had more ups and downs than a giant roller coaster. It will take you through the many near-misses that I have had with fame and fortune.

It is important that my life story be told. Now, you can make your own conclusions when you read one of the greatest stories ever told: *Beyond the Beyond.*

Why would a person who has lived far from a perfect life be the one to be chosen to reveal to the world the greatest mystery in life? What mystery? The mystery of death!

So, strap on your seat belts as I take you through the journey of *Beyond the Beyond.*

ᑲᑯ *Chapter One* ᑲᑯ

It was a cold, gloomy day in the middle of February when I got off my sofa to look out of my living room window. I was so depressed. Snow was falling as big as cotton balls. In a short time, it looked like a couple of inches had accumulated. That is when I decided to pack it in and blow my brains out... and go to the *Beyond the Beyond.*

As I sat back down on the sofa, I was profusely sweating; and at the same time, I had the chills. I started to ask myself if I had the balls to do it, when suddenly I jumped up and walked through the kitchen and down the stairs to the basement. That is where I had hidden a .38 revolver under my washing machine. I bent over and reached under it to get the gun. The sweat was now really dripping down my forehead as I started back up the stairs and into the living room. As I sat down and put the gun into my mouth, I was starting to breathe really heavy.

I was getting ready to pull the trigger—but at that moment, I began to have my last, final thought.

I thought about the time I had saved a friend's life. Then, I began to reflect on what an incredible, crazy life I have lived. That was when it came to me, thinking of all the miracles that I had experienced in my lifetime. I realized that these stories had to be told, especially the last: *Beyond the Beyond.*

I suddenly jumped up off the sofa, took the revolver out of my mouth, and shouted, "I'm going to write a book!" My story must be told. I started to get excited as I thought of all I had to tell. So… here I go!

As I start to write, I think to myself, *Wow! I am fucking nuts. I cheated in grade school, high school, and college. I never read a book in my life—and now, did I really have the balls to attempt to write a book? How the fuck do I accomplish this? I don't even know where to start. What a fucking joke!*

All I know is that the story of the *Beyond the Beyond* is meant to be told.

Let me think! Where do I start? How do I start? It has come to me. I am going to start the book by having you, the reader, help me accomplish writing this book. I think, with your help, we can even make it a bestseller. Wow! Maybe I have something here. Who the fuck ever did this before! Shit, I just got stuck. I don't know how I should continue.

An idea just came to me. If I have you work along with me on this, maybe I can do it. Wow! This might be the answer.

If I close my eyes and I talk to you, the reader, maybe I can do it. Let me try it.

When I was about ten years old, I remember my mother telling me a story about something that took place when I was just a child. In the story, she dropped a handful of pennies on the floor. She said, "Paulie, pick them up for me." When I got on my knees, my nose was nearly touching the floor for me to be able to see where the pennies were. That's the first time she noticed I was almost blind. I was three years old at the time.

Okay, work along with me. I need your help again. Where do I continue? I got it!

It was when I started school and wore a pair of eyeglasses that must have weighed about five pounds, because they were so thick. This is how my fighting began. The older kids would call my glasses Coca-Cola bottles, and I would get so mad that I would beat them up. Before you knew it, I was building a reputation around my town of being tough.

When I was twelve, I was whipping all the sixteen-year-old kids that were making fun of me. It's important for me to say, "I never started a fight or lifted my hands first." The older kids in my neighborhood would go all around the town to try to find a kid tough enough to whoop me, but I beat them all. After a while, they got so mad that they brought in a two-hundred-pound, sixteen-year-old tomboy. They arranged a ten-round boxing match with gloves, me against her. Keep in mind, I was just twelve and about one hundred and ten pounds. The fight lasted until the middle of the tenth round before she quit. Up until that moment, she was kicking my ass. Until this day, whenever I run into some of the old guys, we still have some laughs on how Roseann Otto almost beat me up.

My barber was one of those old guys. Once in a while, when I am getting a haircut, he starts rehashing the story (as he is laughing so hard). In the meantime, the people that are waiting for their haircuts are looking at me in a way as if they're all thinking, "You were fighting a girl!"

Reader, it is important for you to know the strongest belief I always had is that *a man should never raise his hands to a woman!*

I just had a thought on how we should continue this book. This is what I am thinking. As I am going along in chronological order of telling my life story, each time there is a *Beyond the Beyond* miracle, or a funny story, I will stop to tell it.

Here is my first *Beyond the Beyond* story.

I was in the fifth grade in a Catholic grammar school in Lyndhurst, New Jersey. One night, I had a dream that the music teacher, who was a nun, had died. The next day at about ten in the morning, there was an announcement over the loudspeaker that all the students were being released early from school because Sister so-and-so (I do not remember her name) had died. That was the first *Beyond the Beyond* experience I had.

I remember getting the chills through my body as I reflected back to the night before, when I'd had that dream, and then I realized for a short time, I had been *Beyond the Beyond.*

That same year, I remember going to a New York Yankees game. My father had taken me, my brother, John, and our friend, Richie P. The Yankees were playing the Chicago White Sox, and that was Richie P.'s and my favorite team. Before the game started, I told everyone I was going to get a ball. Naturally, they all laughed at me. What were the odds of that? About 50,000 to 1! Then I said, "Yes, it's going to bounce off a seat and hit me in the head." I felt, with every fiber of my body, that it was going to happen. Well! I don't think I have to tell you the rest. Everything happened exactly how I said it would.

We got to the game early. An hour before the game started, the Chicago White Sox were warming up. We were sitting about ten feet past the left field foul pole. The left fielder for the White Sox was a guy named "Jungle Jim" Rivera. He was known for stealing bases head-first. As Richie P. and I were screaming his name, my father said, "Wow, I was in the Army with a guy named Jim Rivera. We were military police together. He was a real good baseball player."

Well, when Richie P. and I heard that, we got so excited that we started screaming, "Jim, Jim, come here!" Sure enough, he walked over.

My father asked, "Were you an MP in the Army stationed in Fort Meyers?"

Jim replied, "Yes."

My father then said, "You don't remember me." Jim looked at my father with confusion. Then, it came to my father that when they had been in the Army together, my father had had a full head of hair, and now he was bald. So, my father said to Jim, "It's fucking Curly!"

When Jim heard that, he replied, "Oh, my God!" as he leaned over the rail and hugged my father. At this time, we were going nuts with excitement, seeing one of our favorite players knowing and hugging my father.

The one part of the conversation that stuck out in my mind was when my father asked him when he was going to retire. Jim replied, "Soon, Curly. It's hard being around these young cunts."

Jim was about thirty-seven at the time, and most of the ballplayers were in their mid-twenties. Before he left us to go back to the dugout, I asked him, "Please, Jim! Hit a home run."

Jim laughed and said, "Kid, I'm a base stealer, not a home run hitter."

I then replied, "Jim, I know that you're going to do it!"

Jim laughed again and answered, "Kid, I'll try."

We were in the seventh inning when my father said, "That's it. We're leaving. If we stay until the end of the game, we'll get stuck in all the traffic."

Well! We were in the car, listening to the game on the radio. It was the ninth inning, and "Jungle Jim" Rivera was up at bat. *I don't have to tell you the rest of what happened!*

At this early age, I first became aware that every time I had these strong feelings and premonitions, there was a special occurrence. What do you think, reader?

I think we should lighten it up a bit with a funny story.

When I'm at a local affair, all my friends beg me to tell this story. This story took place when I was twelve years old. But first, I have to create a little background picture for you. On my street block, there were three friends: Joe "Bug Eyes" or "Bugs," Anthony, and Genardo. Joe Bugs got his nickname because his eyes were as big as light bulbs. Anthony was a good-looking kid who was real smart. Even at the early age of twelve, he knew he wanted to become a doctor, which, eventually, he did. Genardo was a short kid who just got off the boat from Italy and could barely speak English. And then there was me: a tall, skinny, ugly kid with Coke-bottle glasses.

Now, Joe Bugs and Anthony were cousins. Their mothers were sisters-in-law and were always in competition with each other about which kid achieved more. The funny thing is, it was no contest, Anthony was a super-smart, level-headed kid who was never in trouble, while Joe Bugs was not too smart and was always in trouble. Yet, his mother thought he was so much better than his cousin and all the rest of the neighborhood kids.

The story begins when Joe Bugs starts taking accordion lessons. Shortly, after he learns to play about ten songs, he decides to start a band. He gets Genardo to play the drums and a different Anthony, from a few blocks away, to play the guitar. By the way, Anthony was just recently starting to take guitar lessons. Then, there was me. I didn't play an instrument—all my interest was in sports—but, of course, I had to be in the band. So, I became the singer. Oh, my God! I was so terrible, I could not sing in tune at all.

Back to Joe Bugs' mother… She always bragged about her son—constantly. She would be telling everyone how outstanding he was. The funny thing about that was he was such a fuck-up. Shit! I think I already mentioned that. Oh, well, I told you, I need your help to stay organized.

Anyway, Bugs' mother worked in this big company. After two weeks of us practicing, Bugs' mother starts bragging in her company about her son having this great band. One day, when bragging to another co-worker, the president of the company overhears her. Ironically, his daughter was getting married the next day, and at the last minute, the band they had booked had to cancel. The president calls Bugs' mother into his office and started to question her on if we were any good. Well, of course, Bugs' mother starts bragging about her son and his band, saying how great we are. She told him we would do a really great job if he wanted us to fill in. Well, she sold him! I guess he had no choice, being that the wedding was the next night. I think she arranged for us to be paid $200. Remember, this was in 1959, and that was a lot of money!

When she comes home that night from work, we're practicing in her basement. She walks down the stairs with a big smile on her face, telling us we have our first job, and it is the next night. We're so happy and excited, until we remember that we only knew about ten songs, and we could barely play them.

The next problem is that I don't have a microphone stand. Well, I solve that problem right away by getting an old lamppost that's in my neighbor's garbage. Next problem: we need transportation to get to the banquet hall. Problem solved! Anthony's older brother, who was seventeen and had just gotten his license. He said he would drive us to the wedding.

Okay, picture it—this beautiful banquet hall with four hundred guests attending a very elaborate wedding. Remember, this is a president of a big company who's having this reception for his only daughter.

The next night comes, and we get lost. Anthony's brother, who was driving us, didn't know where he was going. He gets us there a half hour late. By this time, it was starting to get fucking crazy in the banquet hall. Both sides of the families are at odds with each other, starting to argue. Just as fists are getting ready to be thrown, all of a sudden, someone yells out, "Everyone calm down! The band just arrived!"

Well, here it is, two hundred people on one side and two hundred people on the opposite side, all getting ready to start battling each other as we walk into the banquet hall.

I can still remember the expressions on all their faces when they see four twelve-year-old kids walking across the floor to get to the stage. You could have heard a pin drop, it was so quiet, as they all looked at us with puzzlement.

Their mouths are wide open when they see me carrying a lamppost over my shoulder. As we get set up on the stage, there's complete silence. Genardo is setting up his drums, Joe Bugs is strapping on his accordion, greenhorn Anthony is tuning his guitar, and I'm setting up the microphone onto the lampshade post. As I look from the

16

stage onto the floor, I notice that not one person has moved, and that it's still completely silent. I start to panic. I know Anthony doesn't play the guitar well, so I tell him not to plug the guitar into the amplifier and just pretend to play. I tell Bugs he has to play the accordion extra-loud so the people wouldn't notice that Anthony was pretending to play the guitar.

Okay! Here we go. You have to picture it. Four twelve-year-old kids—Joe Buggs, with them bulging eyes, squeezing the accordion; Anthony, with pitch-black, greasy hair that looks like it was dipped in olive oil, pretending he was playing the guitar, Genardo with an expression on his face like he was still in Italy and then me, with those coke-bottle eyeglasses, holding a fucking lamppost in my hands.

I start with my back facing the crowd. I turned around and grabbed the lampshade post and started to sing, *I'm in the Mood for Love,* completely out-of-key. Bugs is squeezing the box, Anthony is faking the guitar, and Genardo is banging on the fucking drums.

Well! No sooner do I get the word "love" out of my mouth when there goes the groom's father, running across the room, screaming, "You ruined my son's wedding! I'm going to kill you!" as he starts to throw punches at the bride's father. And then it begins. Two hundred people on one side, two hundred people on the other side, all attacking each other. The women are pulling each other's hair and ripping each other's dresses, as the men are punching each other and smashing chairs over each other's heads.

At about the time I finish the song, the floor looks like the Red Sea. Then, the cops arrive.

I remember, as they're escorting us out of the building, I get up the balls to ask them for our pay. The police officer starts to laugh as he replies, "Son, I wouldn't worry about getting paid. Just be happy that you're still alive."

All right, reader. I have to go back to telling my story. I believe I left off when I was at the age of twelve. One night, I was watching a movie on TV. The name of the movie was *Jim Thorpe—All-American.* It starred Burt Lancaster, as Jim Thorpe. The movie was about the true story of Thorpe's fabulous Olympic running career. After watching that movie, I was so inspired that I started running. Soon, I was running everywhere. The older kids would give me twenty-five cents to run five miles around the high school track.

As I write this, I'm laughing to myself because it reminds me of the movie *Forrest Gump,* with Tom Hanks, and how Forrest was running everywhere as a kid. After a short time, my neighbor, Nicky Pollazzi, noticed and started calling me "the runner", which then became "T.R." It turned out that name stuck with me and started to become popular and, eventually, well-known throughout the state. Every time

I was in the newspaper for athletic achievements in football, track, and boxing, I was referred to as T.R. Everyone knew me as T.R. Most people didn't even know my first name—including all my teachers. When I won the New Jersey State Boxing Championship on TV, I was referred to as T.R.

I was really becoming a good runner. When I was only in the eighth grade, a friend put me in a college five-mile cross-country race. I was winning the race at the four-mile mark until I took a wrong turn and ran an extra three miles. Friends still make fun of me for that!

In my freshman year of high school, I won the Most Valuable Football Player award as a running back. Then, when track season came along, I won all but two varsity races, running the half-mile. I was the only freshman to receive a varsity letter sweater. I was so proud. I wore that wool sweater even in the heat of the summer, in spite of me sweating my ass off.

Of all the races that I ran my freshman year, only one stands out in my memory. It was the first track meet of the season. We were competing against this big regional high school that was famous for their track team. The kid I had to run against was a senior and had won the half-mile state championship the year before. The day of the race, there was no school, so I was building a clubhouse in my backyard with Joe Bugs. I got so involved that I forgot about going to the race.

19

Well! I only lived a couple of blocks from the high school, so my angry coach jumped in his car and came to get me. He dragged me to the track. I won the race, and that was the start of my running career.

Reader, I am starting to feel like a jerk-off telling about some of these small athletic achievements but I think it is important so that you can have a picture of the character in your mind as I tell my story of the *Beyond the Beyond*.

Wow! Right at this very moment that I'm writing these last couple of pages, I just got a phone call. Before I tell what the phone call was about, I have to go back a couple of months. I have a friend who I have been very close to in the past ten years. His name is Richie. Being that I've already written about another close friend named Richie P., I will refer to this Richie as "Richie Cigar," being that he is known for smoking large Churchill cigars. Two months ago he called me and told me he has inoperable cancer and that the doctor informed him that he has a couple of months to live. Well, I sent him a short letter telling of my mother's spirit from *Beyond the Beyond*. I also enclosed one of the medals she had left me. I told him he had to believe in what I said in the letter.

A few days later when he received the letter and the medal, he called. I was not at home, so he left a message which I saved. He tells how he was taken aback by the letter

I had sent and that he truly believed in the spirit of *Beyond the Beyond.*

A week later he called me and told me there was a turnaround and that they could operate. Only minutes ago, as I was writing, I got the phone call. It was my friend crying with joy on the phone as he was screaming, "Your mother's spirit did it! I just came back from the hospital and the doctors say all the tests show I'm cancer free."

The day I mailed the letter with the medal to my friend, there was a lady friend with me. I guaranteed Marie that my friend, Richie Cigar, would be healed, and that she could see for herself the power of the spirit of *Beyond the Beyond.*

I'm going to take a break now, reader. It's time to watch a little TV.

ᏟᎾ *Chapter Two* ᏴᎧ

I am back. As I was lying on my sofa with the TV remote in my hand, flicking the channels, I spotted the movie *Roots*. This is a six-part series, each part being an hour and a half long. Me, being a compulsive person with tunnel vision tendencies, I wind up watching the whole nine hours straight through.

What a great movie! I could not help but shed tears as I watched each episode. The movie was about a time when the American colonials would go to Africa to capture the native people and bring them back to this country to become slaves. From there, it tells the story of slavery in America up to the Civil War.

After watching this movie, I started to look back at my first experience with prejudice. I was twelve years old and would take the morning bus ride on a Saturday to work at my uncle's Italian restaurant. It was in the next town over. One Saturday, a middle-aged black man walks into the restaurant with his son draped along his side. The kid looked to be about my age. The father went up to my uncle and humbly asked if my uncle would mind if his family came in to eat. I remember the sorrow I felt as I looked through teary eyes at the boy's face. Naturally, my uncle said, "I am happy to have you." So, the man called his wife and two daughters who were waiting in the car to come in.

Well! The guilt that I had, seeing that father having to lower himself to ask permission for his family to come in and eat, has always stuck with me.

I remember how hard I tried to make them feel welcomed as I served them. This story had to be told, because there is no prejudice in the *Beyond the Beyond*.

All right, reader, let's get back to my freshman year of high school. Despite the success I had playing sports and the popularity I had from being tough, I was handicapped by being almost blind. The reason for that was that I refused to wear my Coke-bottle eyeglasses. I was too embarrassed to let any girls to see me with them on. So I went through school not being able to see the blackboard.

When I walked through the crowded hallways, I would wave and say, "Hello!" to everyone who passed by, so I wouldn't slight anyone that I should be recognizing.

In my sophomore year, I was playing on the basketball team when a fight broke out between my school and the Lodi basketball team. Players on both teams were fighting out in the middle of the court. I accidentally knocked out the coach of the other team, and that ended my basketball career. During the rest of my high school days, I was not allowed in the gym for a basketball game.

In the meantime, my reputation was building as a tough fighter. It got to a point that the toughest guys from different cities in north Jersey (Paterson, Jersey City, and Newark) would come to my town and look for me. The ones that found me would say they wanted to fight me. They would claim that they were the toughest around. Well! I beat them all. I remember one time reading a newspaper article about me where they said I had over three-hundred street fights.

Many people said I had become a legend in the area as a street fighter. It got to a point that if a guy wasn't twice my size, I wouldn't even fight him. One time I was with my friends at a famous hot dog place in Clifton, New Jersey. The place was packed with about a hundred people in four different lines, waiting to be served, when I overheard a guy from another town telling his friends, "Hey, there's T.R." At that point, a couple of guys anxiously came over to see me. Ha! Like I was some kind of celebrity. That's when I overheard one of them asking, "That's T.R.?" with a disappointed sound in his voice. I was just 175 pounds and a shade under six feet tall.

Well, from that night on, I started my weightlifting and bodybuilding career. Before you knew it, I was 220 pounds, had twenty-one-inch biceps, and could bench-press 600 pounds. That eventually became my profession, which I will come to later.

Despite the street fighting, I was a fun, caring, loving guy in high school. I always protected the weaker kids and never let anyone make fun of them or pick on them. Maybe it was because I knew what it felt like to be made fun of. This point of the story will be relevant when I tell you about the friend's life I saved. I mentioned it in the beginning of the book. Remember? When I was ready to pack it in?

I have to spend more time talking about my high school years since they were the most memorable years. But before I continue talking about my high school years, I am going to stop and go with a funny story. When I keep talking about myself, after a while, I start to feel like a jerk.

Okay… here we go… story time!

It was the beginning of my sophomore year. School had just started a couple of days earlier. I was already skipping class, and I was roaming down the hallways when I heard a lot of noise and commotion coming from this one classroom. When I stopped and looked in the door window, I noticed my best friend, Bobby G. All the kids were laughing and looking like they were having a good time. I let myself into the room, went to the teacher, and asked her, "What class is this?"

She replied, "It's a science class."

I said, "This is where I want to be. I'll be right back." Then I went down to the guidance department and pulled some strings and got into her class. Well, I was able to do whatever I wanted in that class; this teacher didn't care. So I would come every day late for class, and when I would come in, I would get a cup of water from the science sink. This sink had three different spigots.

Well, one day, the teacher sets me up, and she brings all the class in on it—even the school principal and dean. I come into class, and as usual, I go to the sink and get a cup of water. No sooner than I finish drinking the water, this short, stocky science teacher comes diving across the sink, screaming, "T.R.! What did you do? I just told the class before you came in that the water spigot has been turned over to liquid gas and it's toxic!"

While I was standing there, she nervously shouted, "All right, let me think!" She quickly ran to grab this big, thick book. She opened the book and began tearing through the pages until she stopped and said, "Okay, okay, we have to dilute the gases in your stomach. Go outside and down the hallway to the water fountain. Drink all the water that you can, and then come back."

So I did, of course. When I came back, she said, "All right, every five minutes you have to get up and go to the fountain and drink all the water that you can."

In the meantime, each time I would get up and go out to drink the water, the class was going nuts with laughter. Down the opposite hallway, the principal and his entire staff were peeking out and watching me drink the water. After a while, I was drinking so much water that I was starting to get sick. That's when they finally all started to laugh and tell me that the whole thing was a *prank*.

Well, when I heard that, I laughed, left school, and went home and went to sleep.

Oh, shit, before I go too far, I'd better start writing about the first love of my life—the girl who gave me the greatest gift you can receive: four incredible children. We started dating at the beginning of our sophomore year. She was a pretty girl with pitch-black hair, olive skin, and a beautiful figure. The funny thing about her going out with me was she was the smartest kid in our class, and I was the dumbest. All the teachers made a joke about it. She was so smart even the teachers were in awe of her.

Her name was Louise. Being that I was not crazy about that name, I always called her "Hon." Never once in our entire high school years did I call her Louise; it was always Hon. Every once in a while, when my friends were looking to bust my balls, they would call me Hon.

One time in English class, we were given a three-month project to write an essay. Well, all the teachers had always assumed that Hon did all my schoolwork for me. The day the essay project was due, I came into class late because I had to go to my girl's locker to pick up my report. When I walked into the classroom, all the students were already seated. I put my three-month project on the teacher's desk. Ironically, Hon's best subjects were English and literature. She was an outstanding writer. She should be the one writing this book, certainly not me.

Well, when Mr. Joy picked up the report that I put on his desk, he began to browse through the essay. Then he said to me, "T.R., I'll tell you what: if you can tell me the title of your essay that's on the front cover, I will give you an A+." Well, of course, I couldn't. I was so bad I hadn't even taken one minute to look at the front cover. The class had a good laugh that day. The teacher was compassionate enough to give me a D.

Let's go to my junior year of school. After the football season was over, it was the start of my becoming a businessman and an entrepreneur. I started running and organizing these big dances. I had the famous singing groups of the day performing. My favorite was the Duprees. All the kids from all the towns around would come. I was making more money than the teachers, even the principal. I was doing so well that the principal said to me, "T.R. I'll tell you what—help me raise money for the school." I was even raffling off old cars. I would have my close friends posted at the end of each hallway, selling raffle tickets. I even conned the guidance director of the school to let me share his office to run my business.

Anyway, it's my junior year, and track season is ready to start. *The Star-Ledger*, the largest paper in New Jersey, has a half-page article on two kids—me and another kid. The article's about how the paper was predicting all these great accomplishments from us. It turns out, I don't go out for the team because I get this crazy idea that I want to gain weight for my senior year of football. Local people who were following my running career were heartbroken. They would come to my house to try and change my mind. By the way, the other kid in the article became a world class runner in college, and I believe he broke the world record in the mile.

I can't keep talking about my running any longer. It's too frustrating when I think of the possibilities I could have had in breaking so many records.

Let's go to the beginning of my senior year. The football team votes me in as captain. I can't express how much that meant to me. We are getting ready to have our last practice game before starting the season. I have great optimism, knowing that many of the local sports writers picked me as one of the top promising running backs in my area. All those dreams came crashing down with one hit from "Choo-Choo" Coleman. He was a 250-pound all-state lineman for Eastside High School in Newark, New Jersey. I blew my knee out and had to have surgery. This put me out for the entire season.

This was the first major disappointment in my life. I loved football; it was a big part of my life. I could remember how frustrated I felt as I limped for months through the hallways to get to classes. As an overconfident kid, I was shattered. I didn't know if I could ever come back from this disappointment. But by the end of my senior year, my knee had recouped about 95%. So, when there was an opportunity to get into the state boxing tournament, I entered. This was at the time that Mohammed Ali won the world championship, and I idolized him.

Well, I walked into this big hall where all the fighters were. You had to pick a number to see who would fight whom. So, crazy me, I start to imitate Ali. I was screaming, "I don't want to pick a number. I want the biggest, toughest fighter there is here."

Ali's strategy to psych out the opposition seemed to have worked, because half the fighters had looks on their faces like, *I don't want no part of this nut.* It was pretty funny to me.

After winning a couple of fights, I was in the semi-finals, which were going to be televised on this VHF channel. Well, when the word got out, people from all over the area planned to watch me on TV. The fight was held in the Symphony Hall in Newark, New Jersey.

It's the night of the fight. My trainer is taping my hands, getting ready to put my boxing gloves on. It's only minutes away from me leaving the dressing room to make the lonely walk to the ring. As I am starting to climb into the ring, I notice the extra lighting, and I remember that the fight was being shown live on TV. That is when I realized that thousands upon thousands of people were watching me in their homes at that very moment. My childhood dreams were starting to become a reality! I was fighting for the state championship semi-finals.

As I am warming up, the crowd is *booing* me, because I'm going to be fighting a Hispanic kid, and the live crowd was predominantly Hispanic. Well! The bell rings, and I come out fighting, though I've got my hands down by my side. The fans are going crazy seeing this! If I hadn't been so fast, I wouldn't have been able to pull this off. For the first minute of the round, I let him throw all the punches. One of these punches lands on my solar plexus. The pain is so great that I want to go down to one knee just to catch my breath. I'm gasping for air, trying so hard not to show on my face the pain I'm enduring.

When I throw my first punch, it's a hard, straight left jab. I hit him so hard that his nose splits, and the blood splatters into the crowd. The fans are going nuts, seeing me throw only one punch, since that's enough to drop him. When he gets up at the count of eight, I KO him with a left-right combination, and the fight's over. The crowd is *booing* me, and then they start throwing things into the ring. Then, something hits me in the head, and I go totally nuts.

I turn to where it came from and dive headfirst over the ropes and into the crowd. The cops run up and restrain me. They escort me back to the dressing room. The TV announcers are having a field day because of what had just taken place. The next day, my friends are laughing hysterically as they're telling me I looked like Superman flying through the air and over the ropes. I guess it had been funny to see someone my size flying through the air on TV.

A week goes by, and now I am fighting for the championship. The guy I'm fighting was really good, but the way it turned out, he's beat before he got into the ring. He's so intimidated from watching last week's fight that he runs for the whole fight. The fight turns out to be boring, but I won the championship.

The next day in school, the principal gets on the loudspeaker and says he wants to congratulate me for winning the state championship, and that our high school is proud of me as well. I think that my winning the tournament was the reason the senior class voted me Class Athlete, despite my not being able to play one sport my senior year. That recognition was like winning the Heisman Trophy for me. Remember, my whole life was centered on sports.

My high school days were coming to an end. The last couple of years of high school are crazy. You're counting the days for school to be over, and then when it comes, you're sad. I'll never forget the empty feeling that I had on the last day of high school. Here, for four years, I had built this utopia for myself, and now it was over. All the senior guys and girls were hugging each other and crying and saying their goodbyes, wondering if they would ever see each other again. I imagine all the kids everywhere go through this empty, sad feeling as they are leaving high school.

Now, for the first time, I was confused. I didn't know what direction I was going to go in. I didn't have a football scholarship, due to the fact that I missed playing my senior year. The summer was there, and I had to get a job so I can make money for college, even though I didn't have any idea of where I was going. So I, being a businessman, decided to start a painting company. I made my close friend, Bobby G., my business partner. As I am writing this, he is presently the police commissioner of my hometown.

Okay, ready? Here comes a funny story.

Bobby G. and I went out and got these fancy business cards printed up. The cards had our names on them, stating we were president and vice president of the company. We would get all dressed up and go to the local luncheonette, a place called the Valley Sweet Shop. It was a very popular place in our town. We would go there every day and tell people we owned this big painting company, and we would hand out our business cards. In the meantime, we didn't even have a single customer or job.

My father had this small construction company and had just finished some home improvements to this house in our town. So, of course, he said to us, "The homeowner needs her house painted. Go and see her." We had no idea what price to give, so we asked my father for his advice. He said, "Let me see. It should take about four days to complete the job, so ask her for $1,000, and make her pay for the paint." He said we shouldn't do the job for any less.

We went to the house and knocked on the door, and a little old Italian lady answered. She looked about eighty years old. Well, by the time we were through negotiating with this little old lady, we were doing the job for $300, and we were also going to be paying for the paint.

Okay! Picture this: the house started out dark burgundy, and we were painting it canary yellow. Our intention was to start working at 7:00 in the morning each day, but due to the fact that we were out night-clubbing until 2:00 in the morning, we would show up at 11:00 a.m. By the time we got started, it was already time for lunch. We would go home, get dressed up, and go to the Valley Sweet Shop to eat lunch and brag about how we were doing this big job. When we finished our lunch, we had to go back home to put on our work clothes so that we could go back to work. We would only work for about an hour in the afternoon, being that we were so tired from being out the night before. When we decided to wrap it up each day, we would just leave the paint cans and ladders wherever they were. We wouldn't take the time to clean the brushes, so that meant that it would take an hour to clean the rock-solid brushes before we were able to get started the next day. And then, it was time for lunch again. Well, after a few weeks of this routine, our work performance of this painting job was starting to get around town.

Everyone was starting to find our working efforts funny. So, at this point, we decided to have a business meeting. We mutually agreed that we had to get this job done. No more dressing up at lunchtime and going to the Valley Sweet Shop to eat. We were now going to bring our lunch to the job. Our moms would pack us each such a big lunch that we would have to bring it in a shopping bag. Now, when it was lunchtime, we would take the big bedspread that we were using as a drop cloth, spread it out over the lady's beautiful front lawn and have a picnic. About the time we finished that big, heavy lunch, we would fall asleep on the bedspread.

Okay, that wasn't working out. So we decided not to eat lunch anymore. Now, we tried to work during lunch hour, but the little old lady would feel sorry for us, so she started making us lunch. By the time we finished eating the lunch, her elderly Italian lady friends would be over, and we would wind up talking to them all afternoon and listening to all the old stories about Italy and their families from the other side.

By this time, a month had gone by, and we were only half done with the job.

Wait until you hear this part! Remember, I told you the house was dark burgundy and we were painting it canary yellow. As I was painting, I could only stay in the same place for a short period of time, because I would get bored, so I'd have to move to another section of the house. After a while, the house looked like a checkerboard. This house was becoming famous in the area. People from all over were coming to drive by to see the house. At nighttime, there were lines of cars a block long just to see this house.

We finally finished the four-day estimated job two months later. The summer was almost over. By the time we got paid and deducted the cost of the paint that we paid for, we figured it out that we made $1.00 a day. Oh well! That was my first business venture in the real world.

✑ *Chapter Three* ✎

As I am getting ready to continue my life story, which is now going to take us out west to college, I have to stop. The reason is because I decided to call my friend, Richie Cigar. You remember him, right, reader? He's the guy I spoke of earlier—the one who had cancer. I wanted to let him know that I had put his miraculous story in my book. Also, I remembered he'd once told me that he had written books, so I wanted his opinion on how this one was coming along.

So, I began reading to him from the first page all the way up to the last page, where I was getting ready to go to college. I was reading him my life story on the phone. Most of all, I wanted to get his opinion on my so-called funny stories. I wanted to know if he thought they were descriptive enough for them to be funny.

As he began to critique what I had read to him, he asked, "Is this an autobiography, or is it a novel that you are writing?" When I asked him what he meant, he said, "Let me explain. After I wrote my life story in a book called *The Rocking Chair*, I brought it to a publishing company, hoping for it to get published. They told me it was good and well-written, but the reason they would not publish it was because I wasn't well-known or a famous person. They told me that the majority of readers would only have an interest in the autobiography of someone who is well-known."

That scared the shit out of me, though it made sense. But I kept going. Why, reader? All I know is that this book must be written, and that it is destiny for it to be published for the world to read. I have been touched by a spirit from *Beyond the Beyond.*

Here is how I replied to him: "Maybe it's an autobiography of my life, and maybe it's not! Maybe it's a novel about this fictitious character that takes you through his crazy life. Maybe it's a mystery leading you through this mysterious story until you get to the greatest mystery of life: *the mystery of death!* All I can tell you is that the ending will shock the world."

Is this true?

It's up to you, the reader, to decide if this book is an autobiography, a novel, or a mystery. You will have to continue on to see.

Back to my story. There was a pretty close friend of mine that graduated high school a year before me. He went out west to play football at a school called Dixie Junior College. He attended college on a football scholarship and had a very good freshman year. At the last minute, I asked him to call the coach and see if I could have a try-out to make the team. The coach said yes—and that if I did well, I would receive a football scholarship.

It was the middle of August, and I only had a week to get ready to leave, since we had to be at college early for practice. It was about two weeks before classes would start. I was so excited! It was the first time that I would be on my own and away from home. It was also going to be the first time I was going to be on an airplane. I can still clearly remember the excitement and sadness that I felt as I looked out the little airplane window and saw my mom, my dad, and my girlfriend waving goodbye to me from the airport window.

I was going to a small town in the southern part of Utah called St. George. It was only a one-hour ride from St. George to Las Vegas, Nevada, so our flight was to Las Vegas. Wow! What an experience to see the glamour and glitz of Las Vegas—to see the incredible lighting as you looked down the famous strip. It, to me, was really something. Billy and I had to wait about four hours before we could get the bus to St. George, so we attempted to go to a casino for the first time. You had to be twenty-one, and we were only eighteen, but there was no problem—we looked older than our age.

In a couple of hours spent in the Sands Casino, something bad had happened: *We both won $500!*

Why is that bad? Later in the book, you'll see what I mean by that.

Okay, so then we were on the bus to St. George and, for the first time, I wasn't overconfident. I didn't know if I had lost any of my speed from the surgery. But we started out easy, so it was okay. The first day of football practice was just a routine of going through standard drills.

After practice, my friend Billy and I would go into town to this suds place where we had heard all the college kids hung out. When we walked into the place, there were a couple of good-looking girls that were in there. They were really friendly and seemed like they had an interest in us. I guess it didn't hurt that they already knew we were on the football team. The conversation was really going well, until one of the girls jumped up and said, "Look, they're Catholic!" She had noticed a St. Christopher medal around my neck. She acted like we had the plague. Since I had been isolated growing up in a small town, I thought everyone was Italian and Catholic and ate macaroni. This was the first time in my life that I experienced the real world of different religions and cultures.

This was a state that was almost completely Mormon. I remember a few days later a couple of us football players decided to go into town for a few beers. There was only one bar in the entire town, and you had to go in through the back door. We were told this was because if you were seen going through the front door, you were considered a bum, and you'd be considered an outcast to the town's people. Wow! That was really heavy for me to understand!

The next day at practice, the running backs were telling me the times they had achieved for running the hundred-yard dash. The all-American wide receiver claimed to have run a 9.7, while the other backs claimed a 9.8 and 9.9. These times were incredible to me. I myself had never been timed in the hundred-yard dash, and despite me never losing a race in a football uniform, I knew I couldn't run that fast.

That night, I called my father and told him, "I don't know what I'm doing here. These guys are really exceptionally fast."

He replied, "Hang in there, Son. You can do it." My father always believed in me. He was my inspiration in everything I did.

The next day, the coaches came up to me and asked how fast I could run the hundred-yard dash. I told them I didn't know. Well, when practice began, the coach had all the running backs race to see who was the fastest. I almost didn't want to hear or know how fast all the running backs were.

You know what happened? I beat them all!

After the race, the coach called me over and said, "What are you, a wise guy? You didn't know how fast you could run the hundred-yard dash?"

I replied, "I didn't know, coach! I had no idea!"

Well, that night, I was so happy I called my father up to tell him the news. Now, my confidence was back! I thought to myself I was finally going to get my chance. But as the next week progressed, I didn't play one single game. I was heartbroken, but I was never the kind of person to say a word to the coach. My attitude was that I was the fastest running back and as tough as anyone on the field. I should not have to ask to get a chance to play.

I called my father and said, "Dad, I'm coming home."

After I explained why, he replied, "Fuck it. Come on home."

This was the first time I ever quit at something in my life, and I didn't like it at all. It wasn't until many years later that he told me the story of what had happened. He was so pissed-off that he called the coach and asked, "Why the fuck didn't you give my kid a chance? He was the fastest kid on the team."

He told me the coach replied, "We were going to use him for kickoffs and punt returns."

My father said, "I wish you would have told the kid your intentions."

For years, my father never told me this had happened. He knew how mad I would have gotten that he had called the coach in the first place. My belief was that your performance on the field should say it all, no one should ever have to campaign for you to play.

I was home only a week when this friend of my father's told him about this junior college in Yuma, Arizona. He said that he could get me in. At this point, I really didn't want to go back to school, much less back across country, but I knew it was my father's wish that I go to college, so off I went. By the time I got there, it was too late to join the football team.

So there I was, in the middle of the desert, on the outskirts of Yuma, Arizona, in this school called Arizona Western Junior College. I didn't know a single soul, and I was not on the football team. I felt like a nonentity. Looking back to my high school days, I still could remember that feeling of how I used to be so popular—captain of the football team—and how I was always in the limelight. My experience at this little middle-of-nowhere college was a real adjustment and reality check for me.

I had nothing to do, so I started to go to the gym and lift weights. After a little while, some of the football players noticed how strong I was, and we started to become friends.

When Christmas break came along, I went home for a week. I had gotten so big from lifting weights that all my friends back home were amazed. After break, I went back to school. One day, I was with a few friends in the town of Yuma when a Marine sergeant had noticed that I was wearing a windbreaker jacket that said New Jersey State Boxing Champ on it. It was the jacket that I had received from the tournament I won back in high school. We started talking, and then he started arranging boxing matches between me and the Marines from the base a few miles from the college. As the school year went by, I started to get recognition from my boxing matches, and soon I was starting to become very popular on campus.

I would like to take the time to give you an idea of the athletes that we had at this school. First of all, in the little junior college, we had an athlete representing every state in the country. We had football and basketball players who could have gotten full scholarships to all the top universities—such as USC, Notre Dame, Michigan, and Ohio State—if their grades hadn't been so horrendously poor. I am sure there was an agreement between our coaches and the coaches from the big universities to keep an eye on them and encourage them to bring their grades up, and then sway them back to the big schools that wanted them.

Here are a few examples. There was Nate "Tiny" Archibald, who was in the NBA Hall of Fame. He is still the only player in the history of the NBA to hold the record for winning both the scoring title and assist title in the same year. Wow! Do I have memories of him! I remember coming home from my first year summer break and telling all my friends that I had seen the greatest basketball player of all time. When they asked me how tall he was, I told them he was six feet tall. They all started to laugh at me. I remember he came from the ghettos of New York City. He was so poor that he wore the same orange fishnet shirt, green khaki pants, and sneakers with no socks for the entire year.

It's funny when I think of him, because we both had this kind of attitude where we would never say hello to each other. We both waited for the other guy to say it first. Then one night, he came to my room. He was friends with my roommate. He knocked on the door. I answered, "Can I help you?"

He gave me a sneer and turned and walked away. He wouldn't talk to me. I go so mad that I started cursing him out and challenging him to a fight. I was verbally abusive to him, but he kept walking down the hallway.

In later years, when he became famous in the NBA, all my friends would get a kick out of that story. One time, my friends brought me to a New York Knicks game at Madison Square Garden. The Knicks were playing the Kansas City Kings, which was the team that Nate was playing for at the time.

My friends and I were sitting right behind the Kings' bench. As Nate was walking back from a time out, when he got about ten feet from the bench, a friend of mine yelled out, "T.R., Arizona Western College!" Nate looked up, saw my face, and stopped right in his tracks. My friends still tell that story—how they saw with their own eyes that with one look at me, Nate Archibald stopped in his tracks on the floor of Madison Square Garden. But when I look back and think about the cockiness and attitude that he had, I realize that he *needed* that attitude to become a great player.

Let me give you just one more example of an athlete we had at this little junior college: Charley Weaver, a linebacker on our football team. He transferred to USC and became all-American, and then he went on to play in the NFL for ten years for the Detroit Lions.

All right, reader! I have to spend some more time on my college experiences, since I was there for two years. Yuma, Arizona, is about twenty miles from the Mexican border. There's a border town in Mexico called San Louis where all the college kids would go. There were these nightclubs there where you could drink beer and see shows.

Each club also had about twenty or thirty of the most beautiful girls you've ever seen, and they were all hookers. On the side of each nightclub, there were these rooms where you could get laid and get blow jobs. Many of the college guys would go there to get sex—I guess that's the reason I never owned a book in college. When my parents would send me money to buy books, I spent it in Mexico. For three or four bucks, you could drink beer, get laid, and see a show all in one night.

I had this one friend—I really don't remember his real name, but we nicknamed him "Drup" because he got infected with gonorrhea from the whores in Mexico. We would all laugh when he showed us his dick and how the pus would drip out and stain his underwear. This was a common occurrence with many of the students who went to Mexico, but the cure was a simple penicillin shot. I, myself, was lucky I never caught anything.

There was a girl I was dating, and one night, we decided to have a party since her parents had gone away for the weekend. Word spread like wildfire and all the college kids came over. As the evening was getting late, I was in the bedroom with my date. The party started getting wild, and then a fight broke out between some of the football players and basketball players. I jumped up from the bed and ran into the living room where the scuffle was taking place. I noticed three black basketball players out of control. I started to push them and say, "Calm down! We're all friends here."

For about five minutes, heated words were exchanged, but eventually things began to calm down.

There had been tension for weeks brewing between some of the black basketball players and some of the racist rednecks—football players there from Tennessee and Alabama. The problem was that some of the black players were starting to date the white girls. I, myself, had no problem with that. In fact, I felt sorry for those black guys, because there were only a handful of black girls on the entire campus.

Well, the morning after the party, I was going to the cafeteria for breakfast, and all the kids were starting to call out to me, "You crazy Italian!" I really didn't know what they meant by that, until one of the guys who was at the party told me, "Despite the three basketball players having knives in their hands, you were pushing them like you had no fear!"

When I heard that, I really became mad. I thought to myself, *We're all supposed to be friends, and they pulled knives on me.* The truth was it had been dark in the living room. I, with my poor vision, hadn't even seen the knives.

I left the cafeteria and started walking over to the dorm where they lived. As I was angrily walking over, the cafeteria emptied out, and everyone started to follow me. When I arrived at their dorm, the three of them were sitting in the lobby watching TV. I said to them, "You fucking guys had the nerve to pull knives on me. If you have any balls, let's go into the desert, and I'll fight all three of you—one at a time." They accepted my challenge. We walked out of the dorm and started heading for the outskirts of the desert, about 300 yards away. A large crowd of college students who lived on campus was starting to gather.

The first guy I fought, I beat pretty easily. I hit him with a couple of left-right combinations. He went down and didn't want to get up. The next guy I fought was really tough. He was from New York City, and he must have had a lot of street fights, because he knew what he was doing. He was lightning-fast, and he kept hitting me in the face. I couldn't catch up to him until I threw a hard right. I had been aiming for his jaw, but I missed and wound up landing the punch on his shoulder instead. Lucky me! I hit him so hard that I broke his shoulder, but I also dislocated my hand. The top of my thumb bone was sticking out about two inches.

Within a minute of the second fight ending, we all heard sirens blasting. It was the Yuma police and campus patrol, coming to disperse the crowd. Now, remember, there was one fight left to go. This guy was six-foot-six and weighed about 250 pounds. He was from Oklahoma.

It was about noon, and because the cops were roaming all around the campus, we had to postpone the fight until nighttime. I was sick that I had to fight again, seeing the bone sticking out of my hand. Even though I'm sure he did not want to fight either, especially after seeing how I beat his two other friends, neither one of us had a choice. I had to believe the third guy was toughest. This third fight was brewing into some kind of racial thing, and word of it had even traveled into town.

For the rest of the day, my friends were trying to build up my confidence by saying they were going to push the bone back into place and tape my hand. I was really hoping they would have said, "There's no way that we're letting you fight! We're going to take you to the hospital to get your hand treated."

But that didn't happen. Unfortunately, everyone wanted to see the third fight, except for me and the other guy. Both of us had too much pride to back down. I told my friends I wasn't going to be able to fight him in the desert, since the fight was scheduled for 9:00 p.m., and it would be too dark. I wouldn't be able to see him. So all the guys that were involved in the "racial" thing—white and black—made arrangements to have the fight on the football practice field, where there were lights. They planned to break into the sports office to turn on the lights for the field.

In the meantime, things were really brewing in the town as we were coming near to fight time. I remember asking myself how I'd gotten in the middle of all this "racial" tension. I don't have a prejudiced bone in my body.

Oh well! And then, it was time for the fight. There had to be over a thousand people that showed up to see this fight.

The other guy threw the first punch. I ducked and grabbed him. I will never forget the strength that came from his body. It seemed to be supernatural. Now, though, as I look back, I believe he was so scared that I had him in my grasp, his adrenaline gave him that extra strength.

At that moment, the Arizona state police, the county police, the Yuma city police, and the campus patrol showed up to break the whole thing up. After the cops dispersed the crowd, I was the one who sat down with the leaders of the blacks and whites—the ones who were really in the middle of these "racial" differences. We worked everything out, and during my rest of time that I attended that school, there was never another "racial" issue. I did not have enough credits to graduate but I still decided to leave.

It was now time for me to go back home and pursue my dream!

There weren't many opportunities for good boxing matches in Arizona. The one thing I did learn in college from those two years was how to live with people from different races, cultures, and religious beliefs. My father always said there was no better schooling that you could get than the experiences of real life.

My first goal when I got home was to try and prepare for tryouts for the Olympics. A friend of my father's sent me to see a former fighter who had been just seconds from winning the heavyweight championship of the world by almost knocking out the great Joe Louis. His name was "Two-Ton" Tony Galento. With his style, he was considered the toughest street fighter in the history of the sport. My father's friend had taken me to meet him with the idea that when Two-Ton met me, he might want to train me.

Two-Ton said, "Kid, you have to know how to fight with your fucking head." I first thought he meant by always thinking while you were in the ring until he bent his bald head over and showed me all the scars on it. Again, he said, "Kid, you have to know that every opportunity that you get, you have to smash your head into your opponent."

Well, at that moment, I knew he was not the right trainer for me. With all due respect to him, I really thought he was fucking nuts. My entire style and strategy was to hit, and *not to get hit*.

Although I had no intention of having him train me, I decided to train in his gym, which was called Ma Gees Gym. It was located in the back of a bar in his home town of East Orange, New Jersey.

In the meantime, I had to go out and get a job. I remember how frustrated I became looking through the want ads in the newspaper. I didn't see anything that interested me. I became nervous when I started to wonder what would happen if my boxing career didn't work out. What would I do with myself?

One day, as I was browsing through the paper, I came across this advertisement for a physical fitness instructor for this health spa chain. I got excited, because this had really interested me. So, I went to the main office for an interview.

That is when I met a man who called himself Dr. Sorge. He was the president of the company. This guy was flamboyant and exceptionally good-looking. He was an incredibly built man who always wore expensive, well-tailored suits, shirts, and shoes from Italy. He held the bodybuilding title of Mr. North America. He reminded me of Arnold Schwarzenegger, both in looks and build. He was also a good salesman, since he looked like a chiseled Adonis.

Well, I got the job and started as a physical culture instructor for a woman's health spa in Teaneck, New Jersey, and I fell in love with the job! I was helping people get into shape, inspiring them, and motivating and encouraging them to become successful in accomplishing their goals in life.

I loved what I was doing, and I was the best at it. I did have to control myself when I was working with an exceptionally good-looking woman with a gorgeous figure in leotards. A temptation like that was a great way for me to lose focus, but I loved what I was doing so much that I maintained my professionalism at all times.

So, the beginning of my adult life, in the real world, was starting out fine. I was pursuing my boxing dreams and I had found a profession that I would like to spend my life doing.

Then, the biggest tragedy in my life came along. That's when I learned how in seconds, your life can turn around and become something different.

This is what happened to me. I had gone to a friend's wedding on a Saturday evening. After the reception, a few friends who were at the wedding came with me to meet my friend, Bobby G., at the Lyndhurst Diner for coffee. One of my friends was driving, and I was on the passenger side— back then, we called it shotgun—and there was another friend in the back seat.

As we drove into the parking lot, a car was starting to back out of its spot. It almost hit my friend's car. My friend beeped his horn so we wouldn't get into an accident, and then he slowed down and continued into the parking lot.

Someone from the other car yelled out, "Blow it out your ass!"

When I heard these words, I replied in a calm voice out of the window, "Fuck you." I was looking straight ahead as I said those words in a casual tone of voice thinking nothing of it.

By this time, we had gotten to the other end of the parking lot. When my friend parked the car, I started to get out of the passenger side. That's when I saw three angry guys coming towards me, cursing. I said, "Stop! I don't want any trouble!" but they continued angrily coming at me. I told them, "Stop! I don't want to hurt you."

That's when the guy closest to me began to throw the first punch. I blocked it and then threw a punch at him. He went down, hit his head on the ground, and died.

✑ *Chapter Four* ✑

From that moment on, my life had forever changed. The thought of my hands, of *me* being part of the taking of a man's life, has never left me until this day. Now, forty-two years later, when I go to church on Sunday, I pray for this man's spirit.

I was brought to trial for manslaughter.

The support I got from the community was overwhelming. The monsignor of my church, all my friends, and people from my town—they all knew that despite the reputation I had as a fighter, I was known for never *starting* a fight.

Each day of the trial, for the entire week, the courtroom was packed. The entire trial was a sad occasion, except for one moment. The people that were there to support me started showing resentment and dislike for the prosecutor. Most of the people felt this guy was trying, in every way possible, to show that I started the fight, despite all the evidence showing it was not so. I believe most of the people at the trial, including the jury, resented him for his accusations.

So, near the end of the trial when I was on the stand, the prosecutor asked me to get up from the witness chair and step down to the courtroom floor to show him how the punches were thrown. Well, at that moment I was demonstrating how I blocked the punch, and started to pretend to throw my punch. The prosecutor, as he was pretending to be the other guy, was angrily yelling, "Throw the punch! Throw the punch!"

At that moment, you could have read everyone's mind in the courtroom. They were so angry at the prosecutor that everyone (including the jury) started to laugh. In a way, I think that they were hoping I would hit him. At that point, even the judge started to laugh and said, "No, don't hit him." It took the jury just one hour to deliberate before they came back with the verdict: Not guilty! It was self-defense.

It was in that moment that I experienced true joy… before sorrow came back to me, a sorrow that has never left. The night the accident occurred was the end of my boxing career. I didn't want to fight anymore. That one punch shattered all my childhood dreams of someday becoming the world boxing champion.

From the time the accident occurred until the time the trial actually started was about one year. During that time, Hon and I decided to get married. We went to the small town of Elkton, Maryland, to elope. This was a popular place where you could go to get married in one day. We were both twenty-one years old, so we did not need our parents' consent.

When our parents heard the news, they were happy and disappointed at the same time. Our families would have preferred that we waited until Hon graduated college and I was secure in my new career. However, we were both loved by each other's' families. About one month after we eloped, we got married in church, and our families threw us a small, old-fashioned Italian wedding.

So, here I am, twenty-one years old and just married. The court case I had hanging over my head was over and I'm starting my career as a physical culturist in the health spa business. Back then, in the late sixties, the health spa company that I worked for was one of the first of its kind. Many people didn't even know what the words "health spa" meant.

Let's go back to Dr. Sorge, the man who created the company, who also ran the business. The very first glance at him showed how impressive he was in every way. He was operating about ten health clubs when I came into the company. Every Saturday morning, it was mandatory that each of the managers and all the instructors came to a two-hour meeting at the home office which was located in the back of the Teaneck Health Spa.

When you first walked into the main office, you were in this big open room that had six desks. This is where they ran the company. Then, there were twin doors that led into a room with a foot-high platform stage with a podium on it. There were five rows of chairs, ten seats in each row. This is where Dr. Sorge would give these dynamic sales meetings. I remember the time when he told me how he studied Adolph Hitler's speeches. He had the theory that Hitler's speeches were so influential and powerful, that they convinced a country to exterminate millions and millions of people.

Ninety-five percent of the employees that worked in the spa were females. The audience at these meetings consisted of some of the most beautiful girls you ever saw. As Dr. Sorge was putting on his performance each Saturday morning, all the girls were mesmerized by him. I was starting to feel the same, and I started to idolize him. His goal was to keep motivating and pushing the managers to get sales. This guy would strut around holding a cane in his hand. He performed like Gorgeous George, the famous wrestler. He was some showman! He would be talking about the downfalls of eating a hot dog and greasy French fries, but I later found out this was all *fluff*. His main purpose for the meetings was for membership sales. It was sales, sales, and sales. This is where he missed the boat. This was his downfall.

He never maintained the equipment in the gym. Members would always be complaining about exercising machines being broke and never being fixed. The cleanliness of the health club was going downhill fast. It became almost non-existent to have a physical culture instructor available to help the members in their exercise. Back then in was important to have a physical fitness instructor available to show you how to do your exercise.

During this year and one-half in which I worked for this company, Hon and I had our first child. It was a boy. We named him Paul.

Now, the company "Figure Tone," was going downhill fast. This is when I wanted to open my own health and figure spa. I learned all the good parts of the system and had plans to correct all the bad parts. The problem was I had no money—not even a dime to my name. It would take $250,000 to open the spa. That is what I had in mind. When I went to see my father to see if he could help me, he said that the timing was bad. His construction company was not doing well at that time. I began to tell my father that I had a plan that I know would work. The plan consisted of three parts, and I needed his help. It consisted of the following:

(1) A $5,000 loan from the bank.

(2) Ask all of his construction workers if they would work and wait to get paid.

(3) Get credit from the lumber company where he was doing business.

I told him if he was able to accomplish this for me, I had a plan to put together a beautiful health spa with no money (except for the $5,000 loan from the bank). My father saw the belief I had in myself and the faith he had in me.

He said, "I'll get these three things done for you! All I ask of you is that you take your brother, John, in as your partner." John was two and a half years older than me and married with twin boys. He'd had a small men's clothing store in the basement of my father's house for a couple of years, but the business didn't work out.

Well, I told my father, "Yes, I'm happy to have my brother as my partner."

John was a really tough and good football player. He was also really good-looking. I always said, "If I had his looks with my rap, holy shit!" He once had a really good build, but after three years of marriage and not being physically active, he put on about thirty pounds around his midsection. In order for my brother to get involved with me, he had to agree to lose the weight. The plan was to do it over the three months that the spa was being built.

So, here we go into the health spa business. I find this empty cinderblock building in the next town over from where we lived. I make a deal for a ten-year lease and gave the landlord $1,500. We then give him a $500 down payment for PSE&G, the electricity and gas company. Now, we have this big empty building. The first thing I do is have this beautiful office built with a lobby alongside it. We had red carpeting and these gold Roman statues. It was very impressive looking.

The next thing I do is go out and buy a box of chalk.

We had these double cowboy style café doors that would take you from the lobby into the spa. But at this point, when you went through these doors, all you would see is this big, empty shell of a building. So I took the box of chalk and laid out the entire spa. First you entered the gym. Then you would walk through another door to get into the spa area. With the chalk, I drew the sauna, steam, and inhalation rooms. Then I drew a sketch of where the whirlpool and sunrooms would be. You then would go through another entrance to get to the shower, dressing rooms, and makeup area.

I then had these large paper signs made up that read *Women's Health Spa Opening Soon... Half-Price Pre-Enrollment Membership Available.* We put those signs in the front window of the building, and we sent flyers throughout the area. I began to start selling the half-price, pre-enrollment memberships.

As fast as the money was coming in, I was running to the bank to deposit the money into the checking account so that the checks I was writing wouldn't bounce. Every day, I was making out checks to pay for exercise equipment; the sauna, steam and inhalation rooms; the whirlpool and sunrooms; and so much more. I never had a check bounce— not once! Every day, I just kept selling memberships. I was really a good salesman. There was never a woman who walked into my office who walked out without me selling her a membership. I was an artist with words, like a sculptor and painter. I would sculpt their figure and paint them a picture in their minds. I was telling them how we were going to contour and shape their figure and how we were going to tone and uplift their bodies. When they walked out of my office, they were floating like butterflies.

Time for a funny story! One night, as the spa is being built, a lady who I had just sold a membership to is walking out of my office. She's mesmerized by the idea of getting in shape and so excited from what I had told her we were going to do with her. Well, as she's leaving my office, she sees my brother, John, in the lobby. So she asks me, "Who is that?"

I tell her, "He's our head physical culturist."

She replies, "You've got to be kidding me. How could he help me when he can't even help himself?"

Well, I had to bite my tongue so I wouldn't laugh. Here I just got through being an artist, painting this picture for her, and then she sees a heavy, overweight man and is told he's the one who's going to do the sculpting. I soothed her concerns by telling her that he just got married about six months ago, and that's why he put all that weight on, but now he was going to take it off.

I'll never forget the embarrassment on my brother's face. His face was as red as a cherry. From that night on, he started a diet and exercise program that helped him lose that extra weight in two months' time. Because of the embarrassment of that night, my brother has never been overweight in the last forty-two years.

During the construction of the spa, there was a major setback. Hon's mother, who was suffering from cancer, passed away. She was only forty-six years old. She was a good woman, one who I truly loved. When I thought of the love that I had for my mom and dad, I realized what a loss that was for my wife. In the meantime, while consoling my wife and going through the healing process with her, I had the pressure and responsibility of the new business being a success. My entire family's financial future relied on it.

So, here we go. The health spa is opened. I built a half-million dollar health spa without a penny. All it took was a $5,000 loan, a box of chalk, and a belief in me and a dream. I named it New Jersey Health & Figure Spa, even though my father wanted to name it after me: T.R.'s Health Spa or Paul's Health Spa. I wanted to give the perception that the operation was bigger than it actually was. I thought that putting "New Jersey" in the name would accomplish that.

We ran a totally professional health spa. We gave great professional service to the members. We always maintained the equipment and kept the place immaculate. I tried to correct the mistakes that Dr. Sorge made with his spas. Our reputation was so good that we didn't even have to advertise. After just six months, we were doing so well that we paid for an addition to a building that we didn't even own.

A year and a half goes by, and the business is really doing well, when Hon and I had our second child. It was a girl! We named her Gina. I'll never forget the crazy thoughts that went through my mind. I felt that being a father of a girl, I would have to change. I felt I was going to have to set these high moral standards for myself. I felt that if I ever looked at a female again in a sexual way, it would be wrong.

I'll be honest: As time went by, that wore off. Although, since being blessed with a daughter, I've always maintained a deep-rooted belief in the respect for women.

The nervousness that I had when I first started running the health spa lasted a couple of years. The thought of failing had scared me to death. Every night, I would take to bed the fear of not being successful. I tried to work as hard in business as I did in preparing for athletic competition. This is the drive, relating to sports, that I'd had as a young man. My philosophy was always to work twice as hard as my opponent, so I took that with me to the business arena.

It's story time once again! This is the story of the friend's life I saved—the one I mentioned in the beginning of the book. If you remember, the thought of this story was part of what prevented me from blowing my brains out. So, as I look at it, we both saved each other's lives.

One day, about 2:00 in the afternoon, I'm sitting in my office when my secretary buzzes me. She says, "A high school friend of yours is here to see you. His name is Joey."

Not knowing which Joey it might be, I replied, "Have him come in." It turned out to be a friend who had been a year behind me in high school. He had been a small, skinny kid and I always protected him from the kids who always picked on him. I was his hero. Well, this one day he was riding by the spa and realized that I owned it, so he decided to come in and see if I was there.

It turned out to be his final desperate move before he was going to commit suicide. When he came into my office, I gave him a big hug and warm welcome. It was later that day, he told me that the warm greeting that I had given him was the reason he decided to tell me his intentions. He said, "I was on my way to New York City to take an overdose of heroin so that I could kill myself." He then undressed in my office, right down to his underwear. He was nothing but skin and bones. It reminded me of some of the pictures you would see of the Holocaust. It was so hard for me to look at him.

I made him put his clothes back on and sat him down. He started to tell me how he had been taking dope for the past year and it got to a point that he was so bad that his wife had left him about a month earlier. He then started to tell me how he was drinking a bottle of scotch a day. He said that without his wife, he had no purpose to live.

I then began to speak. I told him that I had good news for him. He looked at me like I was nuts. Then, I told him (listen carefully, reader!)... "You are at the lowest point in your life. Looking to kill yourself, you can't get any lower. So, the first thing you have to do is get through today and go into tomorrow. Things could only get better; they can't get any worse. So, here's what we are going to do. The spa opens up at 10:00 in the morning. We're going to sit and talk to each other. We're going to build your mind back up, and then we're going to build your body back up. We're going to do this through exercise, vitamin therapy, and nutrition."

Well, he came in five days a week for about six months. In the meantime, he was off drugs and alcohol. He had physically and mentally built his body and mind back up. Then, one day, I got a phone call. It was Joey! He thanked me for all I had done for him and told me that he was not going to be coming in any longer. His wife came back to him, and he was doing fine.

There is an incredible ending to this story which will take you to the *Beyond the Beyond,* but it will come a little later.

Now, at this time, Hon and I have our third child. It was a boy. We named him Marcus. At this time, I'm working twelve hours a day, five days a week, and Hon was home taking care of three young children. This is when she tells me it's time for us to move out of this four-room apartment and buy a house. So one night, I leave work early and go with her to see this house she'd picked out. It was located one block outside the boundaries of our hometown of Lyndhurst, New Jersey, in a town called Rutherford. As the realtor walked us through the house and to the back door to show us the yard, I couldn't believe my eyes. It was nighttime and it was dark, so when the realtor said, "The back fence is over there," I couldn't even see it! I had to walk to the end of the yard and touch the fence to know it was there. The property was the size of a football field. It was uncommon for any house in our area to have that much property.

So, after seeing the yard and knowing Hon really liked the inside of the house, I immediately say, "We'll take it."

There was a five foot pitch from one side of the yard to the other side the entire length of the yard. We also had five huge, ten-story-tall trees which measured about five feet in circumference at the trunk. The first fall season that we lived there it took us over four hundred giant plastic bags to collect the leaves that had fallen. The town of Rutherford was famous for its old, big trees.

One day, as I'm looking at the yard, I paint a picture in my mind of what I would like the yard to look like. Well, I decided to have that picture come true. What I envisioned would take a tremendous amount of work. Being a little crazy, I decided to do the entire project myself. With a pick, shovel, and wheelbarrow, I leveled the entire yard. I was working twelve hours a day, every Saturday and Sunday. I wouldn't stop to eat, though when Hon would bring me a pitcher of iced tea, I'd take a five-minute break. It took me a year to level the yard—something that would've taken only a day for a bulldozer.

During this time, Hon and I have our fourth child. It was another boy. We named him Brian. We picked that name because, at that time, the movie *Brian's Song* had just come out. It was about the life of a football player who played for the Chicago Bears. Both Hon and I were so inspired and touched by that man, Brian Piccolo that we decided to name our son after him.

Back to the yard! After leveling the yard, I cut those monstrous trees down, took out the tree stumps, and built a five-foot retaining wall the length of the yard. Then on a different level, I put in a built-in swimming pool at the end of the yard. I had large Greek and Roman statues placed in the beautiful rock gardens that I had built.

So here we were, Hon and I and our four children, living in a really nice house with a yard that looked like it came out of a Hollywood magazine. The picture I painted in my mind—my vision of what the yard was supposed to look like—was complete, down to the last final detail. I was so proud of that accomplishment.

In the meantime, the health spa business had been going for a couple of years and was doing well. That is when the biggest downfall in my life started to occur.

ᥱᤁ *Chapter Five* ᥱᤁ

Do you remember my friend, Richie P., from the story of the Chicago White Sox and "Jungle Jim" Rivera? And do you remember the $500 I won in Las Vegas?

One Sunday morning, while Richie P. and I were talking about the New York Giants football game being played later that day, he asked if I wanted to bet $25 on the game. I replied, "You mean I could watch it on TV as I'm eating my macaroni and could win $25?"

Rich replied, "Yes!"

I was intrigued! It was my first introduction to sports gambling.

Shortly after, me being such an optimistic person, thought to myself, *Why bet $25 when I could bet $100? I know who's going to win.*

So, here begins the gambling life of a compulsive person. Throughout the rest of the book, you will hear stories of how this compulsion—this cancer—affected all the creativeness and drive that I had within myself and ruined my life up until you hear the final miracle of *Beyond the Beyond*.

As I mentioned, the health spa was doing very well, and I was building a reputation as a physical fitness guru. When someone would look at me with skepticism and doubt as I was speaking about my profession, I would become frustrated. Soon, I got the crazy idea that if I had the title "Doctor" in front of my name, I would have instant credibility when I spoke. Then, I remembered that Dr. Sorge had this doctorate degree from a special school, so I began to research where I could get a doctorate degree in the field of physical culture and nutrition, as well as preventive medicine.

I discovered a number of home corresponding schools that were giving a diploma of a doctorate of naturopathy. Wow! It was just what I was looking for. This was perfect for me; it pertained to the profession I was in, and it would take a short time to get, even if it didn't have much credibility.

After completing a few of these corresponding schools and receiving a diploma that said Doctor of Naturopathy, the first thing I did was to get a sign to put on my office door that read *Dr. Paul F. Gaccione*. Underneath my name, the sign had the word *Naturopath.*

This was a title that I never abused. I stood totally behind the philosophies of physical culture and nutrition. As time went by, I started to really get interested in naturopathy. I started to research more relating to it. It turned out that the United States Records of Congress had it listed as a recognizable "healing art" founded in the early nineteenth century by a group of medical doctors who didn't believe in pharmacology. Here is the definition of the healing art of naturopathic medicine:

Naturopathic Medicine/Definition of Naturopathic Medicine

Naturopathic medicine is a distinct system of primary health care - an art, science, philosophy and practice of diagnosis, treatment, and prevention of illness. Naturopathic medicine is distinguished by the principles which underlie and determine its practice. These principles are based upon the objective observation of the nature of health and disease, and are continually re-examined in the light of scientific advances. Methods used are consistent with these principles and are chosen upon the basis of patient individuality. Naturopathic physicians are primary health care practitioners, whose diverse techniques include modern and traditional, scientific and empirical methods.

Definition of a Naturopathic Doctor

Diagnoses, treats and cares for patients, system of practice that bases treatment of physiological functions and abnormal conditions on natural laws governing human body. Utilizes physiological, psychological, and mechanical methods, such as air, water, light, heat, earth, phytotherapy, food and herb therapy, psychotherapy, electrotherapy, physiotherapy, minor and orifical surgery, mechanotherapy, naturopathic corrections and manipulation, and natural methods or modalities, together with natural medicines, natural processed foods, and herbs and nature's remedies. Excludes major surgery, therapeutic use of x-ray and radium, and use of drugs, except those assailable substances containing elements or compounds of body tissues and are physiologically compatible to body processes for maintenance of life.

Soon, I found a guy who called himself Dr. Kristoff. He ran a school of naturopathic medicine in Jersey City—or at least, I thought it was a school. It was just fifteen minutes from me. At first, I was so excited to hear the news. I called him and made arrangements to have him come to my office. When he came, I basically found out that the doctorate degree that he was offering was based on the money I could pay for it and not on any academic work to be completed.

After thinking about it for a short time I decided to buy the degree just to have another doctorate degree in naturopathic medicine. Since he was located a short distance from me, I decided to make an appointment to go and meet him. My purpose for the meeting was to find out on what authority, if any, he was issuing these doctorate degrees. Well, I found out! He showed me a charter, which was drawn up in 1920 by an Act of Congress, giving the forefathers of this "healing art" the rights and powers to open a naturopathic college. Under this charter, the power to give doctorate, master, and bachelor degrees in naturopathy, homeopathy, physical therapy, and nutrition were approved.

When I asked him how he obtained the power of this charter, he replied, "I got permission from the family of one of the forefathers."

Since he had this charter, I then asked him, "Why not build a real school of naturopathy?" Remember, I believed in all the principles of what it was all about, and I envisioned what I could do with that charter in a short time. So, I offered him a proposition: I told him if he would give me equal power of the charter, I would find a way to build a college and that, in a short time, it would become something really big. My offer to him was that I would be the Chairman of the Board of Directors, and I would make him President of the school.

He agreed, and so I began. The first thing I did was to bring the charter to some doctor and lawyer friends of mine to make sure everything was legal and in order. The next thing I did was to have a lawyer put in a request to Washington, DC, to change the name from the United States School of Naturopathy to the North America Naturopathic Institute. I also made sure that the new members of the Board of Directors were accepted and on file. There were four people on the Board of Directors; myself, Dr. Matriss, Dr. Kristof, and Al Weinsoff, a lawyer.

Now, through the experiences and knowledge that I obtained in the health spa business, I knew how many people were getting into preventive medicine, nutrition, and the awareness of taking care of themselves. This was in the mid-seventies and this trend was just starting to blossom. The American public was becoming increasingly disenchanted with conventional medicine. The profound clinical limitations of conventional medicine and its out-of-control costs were becoming obvious, and millions of Americans were inspired to look for new options and alternatives. Naturopathy and complementary alternative medicine began to enter a new era of rejuvenation.

So based on the thought that people were starting to believe in naturopathy, the first thing I did was to set up a Booster Club for the new intended school. The purpose of the Booster Club was to have the members, who strongly believed in the "healing art" of naturopathy, plan different kinds of functions to raise money for the new venture. My next thought was that where there are numbers, there's strength.

At this time, we only had a couple of people that were involved. We had my personal friend, Dr. Joseph Matriss, who had his doctorate degree in dentistry. We had a couple of licensed chiropractors and a couple of nutritionists. So, I started thinking about who else I could get involved. I believed that the "healing art" of chiropractic medicine was just a small part of naturopathy. It took me a short time to research and find that most chiropractors were actually practicing naturopathy along with the scientific principles of chiropractic practice. My plan was to start converting more chiropractors, in my area, to join our movement. Since they were educated and practiced a drugless "healing art" already, I issued them each a doctorate of naturopathy diploma from our charter.

As I began to do a little research on both the "healing art" of naturopathy and chiropractic medicine, I learned that both practices were formed and organized in the early 1900s. Back in the mid-seventies, there were only a few books available telling of the forefathers of the "healing arts" of naturopathy. I came to the conclusion that the forefathers of chiropractic medicine envisioned the importance of promoting their "healing art" to the public, but the naturopaths did not recognize this. Obviously, this is why the "healing art" of chiropractic medicine slowly started to get recognized and gain popularity, and naturopathy never really took off. My conclusion was simple. I knew that almost all chiropractors were all using natural, drugless means of helping their patients along with their chiropractic medicines. The science of chiropractic medicine is just a small part of naturopathy. So, based on that theory, my plan was to eventually have all licensed chiropractors also become naturopaths.

Now, after enrolling a number of chiropractors into our movement, I started to set up a New Jersey Society of

Naturopathic Physicians. Each member would receive a certificate to hang in his or her office. I also started a National Society of Naturopathic Physicians. I remember having our first, and only, New Jersey Society of Naturopathic Physicians affair at this beautiful catering hall. I must say, it went well. All of our members were impressed and started to believe in the success of our venture. I remember inviting my father to that banquet and his kidding comment when he said, "I've never seen so many fucking doctors in one spot!" as he began to laugh. He knew that the majority of the people, who attended the banquet, I had made "Doctors" with degrees in naturopathy.

Anyway, my whole plan was starting to work. We were getting ready to look for a building to start a small school. Now, at this time, we were getting people from all over the country to be part of this movement. All of a sudden, I got this phone call from across the country. It was a chiropractor who had joined our organization. He was screaming on the phone. He had checked out Dr. Kristoff and found out that he had been in jail for a lot of serious crimes. When I confronted Dr. Kristoff with these allegations, he did not deny them. When I asked him to resign and he resisted, I decided to put a halt on the entire venture. It hurt me to do this because I had so much faith that I would have succeeded in this venture based on the facts that anything that I decided to do, I had accomplished.

Dr. Kristoff still had equal power in the charter. Since I didn't want to get in any trouble, being involved with him, I decided to walk away. As I look back, I think that if it weren't for the fact that my gambling had escalated and I was starting to lose a lot of money, perhaps I would have hung in there and figured out a way to solve the problem so that the venture could have continued. I have no doubt that if I would have continued with this venture, I would have changed the entire "healing art" of chiropractic medicine, and all chiropractors today would be practicing under the umbrella of naturopathy.

Unfortunately, I've been out of touch with naturopathy since the mid-seventies. I recently took the time to look into where the "healing art" is and where it is going. I was happy to find out that the number of new naturopaths is steadily increasing, and licensure of naturopathic physicians is expanding into new states. By April 1996, eleven states had naturopathic licensing laws (Alaska, Arizona, Connecticut, Hawaii, Maine, Montana, New Hampshire, Oregon, Utah, Vermont, and Washington). A number of other states were likely to enact Naturopathic licensing in the near future.

Naturopathic medical education is growing by leaps and bounds. Three of the four US Naturopathic Medical Schools—National College of Naturopathic Medicine, Bastyr University, and Southwest College—are accredited. The fourth, the University of Bridgeport College of

Naturopathic Medicine, is an applicant for accreditation. Within the past year, all three US Naturopathic Medical Schools and the Canadian College of Naturopathic Medicine in Toronto moved to considerably larger campuses in order to meet the accelerating demand on the part of prospective Naturopathic medical students. In 1996. Bastyr University, alone, had almost 1,000 students enrolled in its various degree-granting programs.

So now, for the most part, my involvement in naturopathy was over, except that I've still got my title of "Doctor." The Health Spa business was still doing well despite my gambling starting to escalate. I was getting so out-of-control (with my compulsive personality) that during basketball season, between college and the pros, I was betting on over sixty games in one evening.

Well! Before I go on, I want to tell you another funny story. I remember one Saturday when the sports office that I was betting with offered a menu of eighty-two games that you could wager on.

This Saturday, the two clerks who were taking wagers over the phones for the sports office made a private $500 bet between themselves. The bet was that they were going to put out a wagering line on Yeshiva minus 3. Yeshiva is a rabbinical college for students who want to become rabbis. They don't have a basketball team! One clerk was betting that I would bet all eighty-two games and would then bet on the eighty-third game that they made up: Yeshiva, minus 3.

The two clerks then anxiously waited for me to call. When I called and finished putting in the last final games, the anticipation was building between the clerks to see if I would bet on Yeshiva. Well, I said "Give me Yeshiva, minus 3."

Then I heard the one clerk screaming, "Yes! I won!"

That is when I found out they were pulling a prank on me and that there was no such wagering line on Yeshiva. Yeshiva didn't even have a team. Oh well! It turned out I only had eighty-two games of action that Saturday, not eighty-three.

I have to stop writing. I'm so angry and frustrated right now. I just got off the phone with my friend, Richie Cigar. Remember, he's the one who had cancer. I've already mentioned he wrote two books. I called him to get his opinion of whether or not I'm making my different stories descriptive enough. He replied to me, "Nobody cares. Nobody cares about your so-called funny stories. Nobody cares about you telling your life story in chronological order. Get to the point! What is *Beyond the Beyond* all about? Is there a message you're trying to tell?" He then said, "You're killing me! I need smelling salt. You're not writing a book—you're writing memoirs."

I answered, "I have the first page to the last page in my mind, heart and soul. Somehow, when I'm finished, it will become a book. I believe, with every fiber of my being, that this will happen. It's destiny!"

Richie then asked, "Are you trying to establish credibility by telling your life story?"

I replied, "No, the complete opposite. I'm trying to discredit myself."

Well! This really got him fucked-up. But I've always done things my way. I don't know any other way. And since I know it's destiny which leads me on this path, I will continue telling my story, my way; and, hopefully, you—the reader—will hang in there.

Where was I? Ah! I'm at my desk getting ready to start writing. My first thought was looking back to Hon and me sitting at the dinner table with our four very young children. Here I had a healthy and loving family for which I was so thankful for. I had such joy and was proud that one of my dreams had come true. At this point in time, I had such a drive in me that I even imagined that I could chase my dream of becoming the World Boxing Champion. It had been about six years that had passed since the accident at the Lyndhurst

Diner. I finally came to terms with myself that boxing was a sport, so I decided to take on this challenge.

I knew how hard it was going to be. I hadn't been in the ring for about six years. I also knew how hard it was going to be to find the time to train. I was working ten to twelve hours a day at the health spa, which left only a few hours for my wife and children, but I had to try. I knew that the way I was going about this venture was totally wrong, but I had no time to waste.

First of all, I should have had a couple of amateur tone-up fights before I turned professional. My second mistake was to be my own manager. The first job of a manager with a fighter of my potential is to research the opponent and make sure he was not a highly skilled fighter at least for the first couple of fights. The idea was that I'd need amateur fights until I got into shape and polished my boxing skills to where they once had been.

My third mistake was I made these two old brothers train me. They were about eighty years old and owned their own gym in Jersey City called Bufano's Gym. They spent a tremendous amount of time training Chuck Wepner (from Bayonne, New Jersey) who fought Mohammed Ali.

When the promoter came to see me at the gym, he immediately wanted to put me on the next boxing card. Being my own manager and knowing I had no time to waste,

I signed the contract to turn pro, even though I was not ready. I had my first match.

Within days of me signing up for the fight, I sold out the arena. The promoter couldn't believe the drawing power I had. He was in his glory.

And then, a couple of days before the fight, I broke my bursa sack in my left shoulder and got bursitis. I remember walking around my dining room table all that night, until the sun came up the next morning. The pain was extremely bad. The next day, I went to the doctor to get a cortisone shot. That night, I met with the promoter, Jimmy Colloto to tell him I had to cancel. He was sick, knowing I had the place sold out.

I told him, "It's no problem. I guarantee you, I'll sell the next fight out."

But he told me my opponent was not any good and with my power, I would knock him out fighting with only one arm. Well, me being my own manager, and with the fighting mentality that I can beat anyone at any time, *he suckered me in!*

My opponent was Ray J. Elson. He was a weightlifting champ from New York. He was very strong and a runner-up in the New York Golden Gloves. This is who the promoter was putting in the ring with me for my first fight, and I was going to be fighting him with one arm!

The day of the fight, I was so mad at the promoter that at my physical, I said to him, "You sign the form that says I'm physically okay to fight. I'm not going to sign it."

The fight lasted three rounds before my opponent stopped me. I almost knocked him out in the first and second rounds fighting with one arm, but I couldn't finish him off.

After the fight, he and his famous trainer, Patty Flood, came to me and said, "We couldn't believe how strong you are! We almost quit."

As I look back to that fight, I get some satisfaction to think if I had done things right, it might have been me fighting for the World Championship.

Well, Ray J. Elson went on to win twenty-three consecutive fights, undefeated. He fought on TV twice for the light Heavyweight Championship of the World. His first championship fight was against Joya Auhmatta. He almost won. It was a very close fifteen-round decision. His second title fight was against Michael Spinks, the greatest light Heavyweight Champion ever. That fight, he was knocked out in the first round!

I could never talk about this fight or the story behind it. No one but my family, and my friend, Richie P., knew about my shoulder.

By the way, there's a crazy ending to this story. I just realized it a couple of years ago, when I was at a block party that Richie P. was having for all the guys who grew up in the neighborhood. That night, the guys brought up the story of that fight. For a few laughs, I told them about our friend, Jimmy Mallacio, who I made my assistant trainer, and how he had talked me into going to an X-rated movie theater to watch porn on the day of the fight. He said it would relax me. Well, we got there at noon and stayed there until 6:00 in the evening, before we left to go to the arena. Looking back now, I realize that I had sat there for six hours with an erection. That was physically exhausting—equivalent to having intercourse for six straight hours! I remember when it was time to get up to go to the fight, I could barely walk, I was so physically spent. It's funny that all those years had gone by and I never realized that mistake.

Now, I realized that there was no way that I would have the time which is needed to seriously pursue my boxing dream. I put all my effort back into the health spa. A few months go by, and I get this phone call from a man from New York. He tells me that he heard about my expertise in the health spa business and he had a friend who is looking to open up a million dollar spa in Puerto Rico and he is looking for some good advice.

The person turned out to be Orlando "the Baby Bull" Cepeda, from the San Francisco Giants. He had just retired from baseball and was in New York to play in his first Old Timers game. We made an appointment for him to come to the health spa to meet me. After taking a tour of the spa, we went for lunch. After lunch, we had a meeting. We made a deal that I would receive $50,000 to go to Puerto Rico and help design the spa, as well as giving him my system and my expertise. As part of the deal, he threw in some free publicity that he was going to get from *Sports Illustrated.* The magazine was going to be doing a story on his retirement.

After our business was completed, I remember Orlando discussing the difference in the working efforts, in his opinion, between Cubans and Puerto Ricans. He had such sadness in him that he started to cry. Here was this physically big man showing such emotion. Right then, I saw that he had a special light in his soul.

So, the deal was made, and I planned my trip to Puerto Rico the following month to get started. A few weeks go by when I receive a phone call from my friend, Richie P. He asks, "Did you see the front page of the *Daily News?*"

I answered, "No." He then said, "I'm not going to say anything. Go out and get the paper and call me back."

Well, the headline story was that Orlando Cepeda had been arrested for drug smuggling. I was sick. Here I was going to receive $50,000 to put towards opening my next health spa, not to mention the publicity that I was going to get from *Sports Illustrated.* All that went down the toilet.

ᴄ⁄ᴏ *Chapter Six* ᴄ⁄ᴏ

I started to write this book in the middle of February 2010. As I pick up my pen, and continue to write, it's 5:00 in the morning, April 8, 2010. I have to stop telling my life story for a moment because of a recent occurrence. I have to go back a few days to Monday, April 5. This was the day before my mother's birthday, April 6. My mother left this world February 28, 1993.

The day of April 5, I get this strong premonition that something is going to happen on her birthday. Then a thought came into my mind: I'm going to play her birthday 006 with the New Jersey pick-it. Ironically, despite me being a big sports gambler, I've only played the pick-it a handful of times. In fact, it's only been four times in forty years. My feelings were so strong that I told my nephew, John; my girlfriend, Marie; and her mother. I told them that something has come over me, and I feel like I can guarantee that my mother's special number, 006, was going to come out on her birthday. I tried to call my two brothers, John and Mark, to tell them what I believed was going to happen, but neither one was home.

There was one other person that I thought to call, but decided not to. That was my friend, Richie Cigar. I thought he would really think I'm nuts. Besides it was only a couple of days earlier that he got annoyed with me about how I was writing the book.

One more point on this, reader. The people I just mentioned are the only people that know that I'm writing this book, and they only have the knowledge of where I'm up to in my writings. At this moment, no one knows what *Beyond the Beyond* is all about.

So on Tuesday morning, April 6—my mother's birthday—I go to play her number 006. The man at the store asks me, "Do you want it for the daytime or for the nighttime?" I thought to myself, *I don't want to spend twice the money by playing the number both daytime and nighttime. But if my feelings are true, I will be able to pick when it will come out.* My feeling was to pick nighttime, so I did just that.

That afternoon, I said as I looked up, "God, I know I need no other signs for me to go forward with my story of *Beyond the Beyond*, but if I could get one more sign from my mother's spirit, to reinforce to myself that I'm not nuts or delusional, I will find a way for this story to become a book for the world to read. I have no idea how I will accomplish this, but I know with every fiber of my being, that it will be done. It's destiny!"

The pick three results come out live on TV at 8:00 p.m., but on the night of April 6, I was so involved in writing this book that I forgot to go check the numbers. When the eleven o'clock news came on that evening, I decided to go to sleep. I always keep the TV on, with the volume turned down low, throughout the night. Well! I'm in a sound sleep, when suddenly about 3:00 in the morning I awaken. At that very moment the news is on the TV, and they are showing the results of the winning number for earlier that evening. The pick three was 006.

I began to cry, and my heart felt like it was going to bust out of my chest, but I didn't care. I called my nephew, John, and my kid brother, Mark, and woke them up. I got them to come over to my house to share the experience with me of what had happened. It took me eight hours to get up enough curiosity to see how much I won. Although I could have really used the money, the $1,400 that I had won meant nothing. I was told it was an exceptionally high payout for the pick three.

What were the odds? I hadn't played the pick-it in five years, and yet I played it on that day. What was the probability for my mother's birthday number to come out on her birthday? What were the odds that I would know that it was going to come out in the evening, and not in the daytime? What were the odds for me to awake out of a sound sleep at the very moment that they were showing the results of the winning number? What were the odds that I asked a higher power for one more sign—even though it was not needed—only to have that sign granted?

Now think, reader! What are the odds of all those different scenarios happening at the same time? As incredible as this may sound, it's just a small story as I take you through this journey, but as you go along you will see the relevance of this.

Anyway, back to my life story.

Atlantic City had had casino gambling for a year when I first went there. I had lost a lot of money that week betting on sports, and only had half the money to cover my losses. So I went to Resorts International Casino in hopes of winning some money. Wow! Was that a mistake!

Resorts was the first casino built in Atlantic City. The first few years, they were the only game in town. I remember reading a newspaper article saying that Resorts was grossing more money than two-thirds of all the casinos on the strip in Las Vegas. You had to see that place the first couple of years that they were open. There was so much action that they allowed customers to bet behind the players that were sitting playing blackjack.

Well! That first trip was the start of me living in the casinos for over thirty years. I believe I hold a few records down there, which we will eventually cover.

At this time, my gambling was now starting to escalate. I was gambling on sports and gambling in the casino in Atlantic City. One week, I had lost betting on sports, and I didn't have the money to pay the bookies. There was a woman who was a member of the spa that I had become close with. So I asked her for a $5,000 loan, which she gave me. Her name is Angie. Remember her—she eventually will become a big part of my life.

Now, for the first time in my life, I was losing at something, and I didn't know how to accept defeat. I was starting to go downhill, but not enough at this point to self-destruct. I still had a clear enough head to maintain some of my creativeness.

So, at this point, I get the idea that I can revolutionize the sport of boxing. My idea was to bring the sport of boxing, not only to a one-on-one competition, but to bring it to a team competition. Here was my theory. It was the mid-seventies, and the NFL was at the height of its popularity. People were really getting into the physical roughness of the game. Boxing offered that same physical competition. I decide to start the National Boxing League, and structure it exactly like the NFL.

Each major city would have its own team. Each competition would consist of ten matches, each match being four rounds. The bouts would be held at the same arenas that the NBA used. After each bout, the winner would receive either three points for a knockout or one point for a decision. There would be a score board, so after each bout, the score change between the two cities that were in competition. Fans could not only root for a fighter, but they could root for their favorite city's team.

Just like the other pro sports leagues, I knew that for this idea to work, I would have to get one of the three major TV networks to buy the deal. At the time, the ABC Sports Department was destroying NBC and CBS, and everything that ABC touched was becoming really successful. The heads of NBC and CBS were really putting pressure on their sports departments to try and be more competitive. They were trying to come up with new ideas and concepts. The TV ratings were really lopsided, with ABC winning by a mile.

My strategy was to bring my plans (when I was ready) to both NBC and CBS. I felt that they couldn't risk letting something this good go by. They were not going to be able to risk ABC picking it up. My plan was to do this venture similar to the start of the health spa, with very little money, even though this was a monstrous endeavor.

I told my brother, John, "We'll take some money from the spa to try and get this venture off the ground, and if we're successful, we'll be partners." I made up a prospectus and sent it to all the different sports franchise owners. I also sent it to some of the famous boxing trainers. The only person I didn't send it to was Don King. At the time, he was controlling much of boxing, and he was making so much money that I thought not only would he not be interested, but he would try to somehow squash what I was doing. I figured that he wouldn't want any new concepts to the sport of boxing when he was doing so well the way things were.

We started this venture out of my office in the health spa. I designed this big beautiful banner. Our logo was similar to the NFL's logo, except we had NBL on it, and on the top of the logo, instead of a football, we had a pair of boxing gloves.

The next thing I did is have another phone put in for the NBL. I'll never forget the first call I received on that phone. When the phone rang for the first time, I answered, "National Boxing League." The person calling was Floyd Patterson, the former heavyweight Champion of the World. Someone had given him our prospectus, and he told me that he was very interested. He had been my first boxing hero as a kid.

Well! We made an appointment for me to meet with him and his lawyer at his home. He lived in New Paltz, New York. Before the day of the meeting, I got the idea that since he was so excited and interested in this new venture, I could offer him the position of commissioner of the new league. I figured that would give us instant credibility.

I'll never forget the day I walked into his home. Here I am, a twenty-eight year old guy, and I'm in a former heavyweight champion's home! As he walked me into his den, my thoughts went back to those days of watching him on TV, fighting his championship fights. He showed me his trophies and then the world championship belt. When I held that belt in my hands, I thought of all my childhood dreams that someday that I could have won that belt. Wow! That was really something.

Okay, let me get back down to earth. So Floyd, his lawyer, his wife (Janice), and I sat and had lunch. I remember as we were eating lunch that I told them a story. It was a story my father's friend told me. Here's the story:

My dad's friend was the trainer of a kid in the amateurs. In this one fight, in the very first round, the kid is getting his ass kicked, when the bell rings for the minute's rest, my father's friend is telling the kid that he's doing a great job and for him to keep up the good work. In the second round, he's getting the shit kicked out of him. His face is all busted up. At the end of the second round, again, my father's friend starts telling the kid how great a job he's doing, and that he should keep up the good work.

Well! The bell is getting ready to ring for the start of the third round, and then the kid says to my father's friend, "Do me a favor: Keep an eye out for the referee, because *somebody* is punching the shit out of me."

Floyd and his lawyer got a laugh out of that, and that made me feel comfortable. Well! That meeting went well, and Floyd was seriously considering coming on board. In the meantime, we were starting to get people that were seriously thinking of investing, when all of a sudden I see on TV that

Don King is going to be starting this boxing tournament. I believe he called it the United States Boxing Tournament. He brought his idea to ABC, and they jumped right on it. It only lasted a couple of weeks before ABC cancelled it. The reason was that there were claims that there was falsifications of the fighters' records, and that the fighters had to give kickbacks from their purses. ABC dropped it like a hot potato.

That put the damper on my venture. After that, nobody wanted to get involved with boxing.

A year goes by. My gambling problem is getting worse, and I start to cheat on Hon. I make arrangements to go to Las Vegas with Angie, the woman I mentioned that was a member of the health spa, and the one I borrowed the money from. As we are getting seated on the plane to Vegas, Angie says, "Oh, my God! Look at that big man and his hair." When I looked up and saw it was Don King, I was shocked. He was sitting in first class, and we were in coach.

I had to go talk to him, so I went into first class where he was sitting. There was a seat open right next to him so I sat in it. I then said to him, "I don't know if you know my name. I'm Paul Gaccione, the guy who was trying to start the National Boxing League."

He replied, "I know of you."

Then I asked him, "Would you admit that you got some of your boxing ideas for the US Boxing Tournaments that you had started from me?"

He said, "Yes."

I knew it, he had gotten my prospectus from one of the boxing trainers that we had sent it to. I then said to him, "If I would have brought this idea and concept to you, would you have invested and become my partner?"

He replied, "Definitely, yes."

It turned out that I outsmarted myself by keeping this from him. I thought there would be no way he would be interested in anything new when he was doing so well the way things were. But when I think back now, I see that I was wrong. He was a real high roller, a real entrepreneur, a guy that wanted to take on new ventures. As I look back and think if I would have gone to him, with the connections he had with the TV networks and the millions that he could have invested, I have no doubt this would have become a reality.

When Angie and I arrive in Las Vegas, we go to see a show. Don Rickles is performing and, where we were sitting, our elbows were touching the stage. During the show, he calls Angie to come onto the stage. He asks her name, and she answers, "It's Angie."

He goes on to do a skit with her, and when he goes to say her name, he calls her, "Andrea."

I told him, "It's not Andrea. It's Angie."

So he tells me, "Come on up here. What's your name?"

When I tell him my name, he drops the microphone, starts to shake, and walks over to the piano, where there's a box of tissues on top. He starts pulling out tissues and puts them in his mouth, on both sides of his jaw. Then he goes into a Godfather skit.

When he finishes up, he bends me over and starts kissing me on the lips, and that's when I realize he has his mouth open from all the tissues stuffed in it. I pull him off, and he goes flying across the stage. Then he buys us a bottle of Dom Perignon for being good sports.

Now, my gambling is really getting me fucked-up. I'm starting to go out with Angie for mental relief and then I start getting emotionally involved. That really starts fucking me up. Here I have a wife, who I truly love and admire, and four children that I love so much, and I'm falling in love with another woman at the same time.

The gambling cancer is affecting me, but still not to the point that I cannot function as a businessman. So my brother, John, and I decided to open another spa. This one was going to be a men's spa. We buy an old A & P supermarket building and turn it into a beautiful men's spa. We had this beautiful lobby and lounge with a fruit bar.

The new spa was a success, but not really what it could have been if the gambling cancer would not have progressed. One day, my father, John, and I were sitting at the counter of the fruit bar when my father glanced at this big tree in a planter that we had in one corner of the lobby. My father said to us, "I'll be a son of a bitch. You see that big tree? For two years, every month, I'd get ready to throw that fuckin' plant out. All the leaves fall off it, and it looks like it's almost completely dead, and then all of a sudden out of nowhere, it comes back to life—all the leaves come back, and it becomes so vibrant."

Then my brother, John, says, "Holy shit, Dad. I can't believe what you are saying. I noticed that the last two years myself, and couldn't figure it out."

Then I said, "You guys are right. I noticed it too, but never gave it a second thought." Then I realized something, and said, "Wow! Oh, my God! Do you guys remember where that plant came from? It came from Joey, the kid whose life I saved! Remember the kid who was going to commit suicide? He sent us that plant for our grand opening. The card read *You gave me life, and now I wish you good luck in your new business.*" Then all of a sudden something came over me, and I said to my dad and brother, "His living spirit sent us that plant to remind us that he was near death and he was brought back to life." My father and my brother were truly touched and believed in what I had said.

After the second year of us having two health spas is when my life gets really fucked up. My plan was to start opening health spas all throughout the area. The health spa business was just starting to become popular, so my plan was to try and dominate the industry. But all those plans were not to be. My gambling cancer had progressed to the point that I was losing so much money that I had to sell both health spas. In the meantime, I had fallen in love with Angie. This was the worst part of my life. I still loved my wife. I knew what a great person she was. I knew how loyal she was and what a great mother she was.

Between the pressures of gambling and having to sell the business, and being in love with both my wife and Angie, I was really fucked-up. My wife was putting pressure on me to quit gambling, and I couldn't do it. I just could not accept defeat. I could not accept all that I had lost. My positive personality said that somehow, I would get it back. I had to keep gambling. So I moved in with Angie. The guilt that I had for leaving my wife and children has never left me.

Now! I was trying to put in my mind that many people get divorced and both Hon and I would adjust. I had hoped that I could still have a meaningful relationship with my children, but the guilt that I had after leaving my wife affected me from being around my children. I truly love my children with all my heart, but the guilt I felt made it hard for me to face my children for that first year that we were separated. I was a weak person at that point of my life, and a piece of shit.

Now! I was at the point that I was gambling like a complete crazy man. The pressure that I would put on myself from gambling was helping to smother my guilt of leaving my wife.

So now, at this time, Angie and I are going down to Atlantic City Resort's Casino every week. I'm considered a high-roller, because of the action I was giving them. We were staying in beautiful penthouse suites, seeing all the top stars perform, and eating in gourmet restaurants, all complimentary. Big deal! Compared to the fuckin money I was losing every week, the comps were a joke.

Now I started borrowing money from family and friends. Never once did I ever borrow money from anyone that I didn't intend to pay back. When I could, I would pay back. But the gambling cancer steadily kept putting me in debt. At this point, I tried going to Gambling Anonymous, but I was weak.

I couldn't face the people that I borrowed money from, and couldn't face the fact that I would have to tell them they would have to accept small amounts of money each month for years and years to pay back the money they had loaned me. So I just kept chasing the dream that I would make a big score fast, pay off all my debts, and have some money left to get a new start. For about two years, I was chasing that dream, week after week.

So one day, after other losing trip, I was packing my suitcase. I had just lost a lot of money, and I was telling Angie, "I can't do this anymore. I have to quit. I cannot take it anymore." At that moment, Angie put the TV on. I'll never forget: It was a Philadelphia station, Channel 10, showing a talk show. The guest was a guy named Kenny Uston. He was the world's greatest card counter. From what I remember, I think he was the Vice President of the Pacific Stock Exchange in San Francisco. Kenny was one of those highly intelligent guys that had put together a system to beat the game of blackjack.

Well! On the show, he was telling how he has left his job and how he had won millions and millions of dollars in all the casinos in Las Vegas, Atlantic City, and all the casinos throughout the world. He then was telling about the book that he had written explaining how he had done it. He then was telling how all the casinos had barred him from playing anymore. He then went on to tell how he would try for a while to wear disguises to go into the casinos.

Later in the show, he had mentioned that he was living in a condo, on the corner of Mortimer Avenue and the boardwalk in Atlantic City. Well! When I heard that, I picked up the phone and made a call to a friend that knew everyone in Atlantic City. I asked him if he could get me an appointment with Kenny Uston as soon as possible. He replied, "I'll call you back tonight." Sure enough, I got the call that night. My friend said, "You have an appointment to meet with Kenny, 9:00 tomorrow morning, for breakfast." I was happy until I realized that he would have to pay for breakfast, being that I was broke!

We met for breakfast, and I started telling Kenny how I was losing so much money playing blackjack. I also told him that I was a young successful businessman who lost his business from sports gambling. He then asked me, "Are you a good blackjack player?"

I replied, "Yes, I'm good."

He then asked, "Do you mind if I give you a test?"

I said, "No, not at all."

After I took the test, and flunked, I was sick. I think I got a score of forty, with one-hundred being the best. I thought to myself, *"Here I've been losing thousands of dollars playing , thinking I was a good player, and now I find out that I was really a bad player."*

I then talked him into teaching me his card-counting system—the plus/minus system and what the risk factor of your bankroll was all about. He showed me how the units wagered would determine what the risk factor would be to your bankroll. He then made arrangements to meet with me numerous times to teach me his systems. That system would determine the odds that I would reach my money goal that I set, *before* I could lose my bankroll.

I'm not going to spend any more time going through all the intricate parts and variables of the system. The bottom line is that I studied hard and practiced a lot, especially since I knew I was not very smart. Numbers and mathematics have always been my real weaknesses.

Well! I put together a bankroll, and I started. Part of the system is you would have to have a cut-off point for each trip. I set a one-week, seven day cut-off. That meant if I didn't reach my money goal by the seventh day, then that trip would have to end, and I would start fresh the following week. Well! I won $5,000 every week, for fifty straight weeks. That was net. I had about $2,000 a week in expenses that the casino would pick up. Each week, the time it took to reach my goal had differed. Some weeks it was three days, sometimes five days, and sometimes it took all the way to seven days.

But I always hit my goal before the cut-off time. Every week, for those fifty winning weeks, I just saved almost every penny. I kept building my bankroll up. My goal was to build a big enough bankroll to really get back on my feet, and then to take care of all my debts and financially take care of my wife and children.

Things were finally turning around. I remembered saying to myself, *"Gambling almost took me down, but I found a way to beat it!"* I was so proud of myself. On the fifty-first week, Angie couldn't make the trip—she had something personal to take care of—so I went to Atlantic City alone. She asked me, "When will I see you?"

I told her, "You know the routine—maybe in one day, maybe in seven days, or maybe one day in between." The way it turned out, I hit my $5,000 mark the first day—in fact I won a couple of hundred over the mark. That day, the mathematical count was so high in my favor, that if I was wagering with a really high risk factor, I would have won $100,000 that day. So I call Angie and tell her, "I hit my mark. I'm coming home. Put on a fresh pot of gravy—I'm wishing for pasta! I'll be home in a couple of hours."

Well! As I'm walking towards the cashier to cash in my chips and to go get my bankroll out of the safe deposit box, I'm passing by the roulette tables. I say to myself, *"I have a couple of hundred, over my mark that I have won. Let me take a shot with that couple of hundred, and see if I could get lucky."* There it was! I dropped my guard for the first time in a year, and started to gamble. The first few minutes I got hot, and my numbers were coming out. I won $8,000 real quick, and then $16,000, and then $80,000. The blood was rushing to my head, and I said to myself, *"This is it! I'm going to win back all the money that I lost in gambling through the years, all in one day, and it's today."*

I dropped my guard, and I became a crazy gambler.

It turned out that I lost every penny that I had won playing roulette that day. Then I started to gamble with my entire card-counting bankroll playing roulette. I stood there for two straight weeks gambling on roulette until I lost every penny that I had worked so hard for over the last year. The bottom line is that a professional card-counter could never drop his guard and become a gambler. But I did. I dropped my guard and let that happen. When I got home two weeks later, I looked up, and said, "No, I didn't beat gambling. Gambling has beaten me." I found out a few years later that Kenny Uston had died at the early age of forty-two. I think it was from cancer.

Resort's Casino in Atlantic City was still rocking and rolling. The action they were getting was unbelievable. The year that I was card-counting and playing in Resort's famous pit—this was a special room where all the high rollers would play—I remember playing with many wealthy, really successful businessmen from Philly and New York. Many of them got caught with their guards down and lost most of everything they had. These were guys who were older and much smarter than me. I remember seeing on television, on CBS' 60 Minutes, a story they were doing on Leonard Toss. He was the owner of the Philadelphia Eagles' NFL football team. The story about how he had lost so much money in Atlantic City that he had to sell the football team. I used to play with him all the time. I also remember playing with a guy who was the biggest diamond business man in Philly. He was a multi-millionaire, until he went broke. From what I remember, he blew his brains out. Those first six years that Atlantic City had gambling, it would be hard to believe how many smart, wealthy businessmen went down for the count and were knocked out.

As I look back, I believe many of them went down to the casino with their guards totally down. They got caught up in the glamour and glitz, and all the attention and VIP treatment that they were given. Then, as they started to lose, their egos took over, and they didn't know how to stop. The bottom line is that people should never drop their guard when it comes to gambling.

After I screwed up my card-counting venture, I started exclusively playing roulette. For the next couple of years, I was playing more hours of roulette than anyone in the country. Many times when I would be playing, the security guards would rope off the section that I was in.

At this time, my children were at the age where they are starting to play little league baseball, football, and basketball. It turned out that they excelled in every sport. I was very proud, but I knew in my heart that if they were not good athletes, it would not have mattered. I was aware that just for kids to participate in team sports was beneficial to their growth. I remembered seeing kids' fathers embarrassing themselves and their kids when they would be complaining to the coach, asking why their kid wasn't playing more. They were doing more harm to the kids than helping. When my kids started playing sports, it helped me to bond with them, despite me still having psychological hang-ups about my separation.

Soon, I began to get this strong spiritual feeling that had come over me. I'm a Christian. I believe in Jesus Christ. As far back as I could remember, I was always spiritually moved when I heard the story of the life of Christ. From when I was a little boy up to this very day, I have always been teased by friends and family because I've always watched all the holy and biblical movies, each one over a hundred times.

Since I was young, I would get these strong feelings that my calling was to preach the life of Christ. I believed that I had a special gift to be able to touch people when I spoke. Every time I got those feelings throughout my life, I immediately dismissed them. When I looked at myself and saw what an imperfect person I was, I realized I could never be a fraud and preach Jesus' teachings and be a sinner. I have never spoken of these feelings to a single soul until now.

It was 8:20 a.m., April 20, 2010, when I heard a loud bang on my door. I was already a couple of hours into working on my book. As the banging got louder, I stopped my one-finger pitter-patter on the typerwriter and got up to see who was at the door. I walked down the kitchen stairs to open the side door. Through the window, I saw a middle-aged, thin and muscular, tall man dressed in casual street clothes with a gun holstered at his side. He said, "FBI, open the door." I opened the door, and my heart started pounding as about fifteen law enforcement officers barged into my house. After they had all entered, you could barely walk in the kitchen, there were so many bodies.

As one agent cuffed me to the chair, another agent told me I was being arrested for murder. He mentioned a name—I had no idea who it was. The different agencies that were represented at the arrest were the FBI, the state of New York, the county sheriff, and the Lyndhurst police. I was so embarrassed to see the police chief of my home town had to be part of the arrest. I remember as the FBI agent was talking to me, I was paying more attention to my police chief looking at my boxing picture on the kitchen wall. I was well-known in my home town, and like to think I was respected as a good guy. I believe he kind of looked up to some of my athletic achievements.

My first stop was going to be my home town jail until the county could come and pick me up. It was awkward to be in my home town police station. The police chief said that he felt sorry for what just had happened. In turn, apologized to him for the commotion I caused the town that day with the arrest. Now, I was sitting in a cold, gloomy jail cell, waiting to be extradited to New York, where they say the crime took place. I was annoyed and depressed that my family and friends would have to read these horrible accusations in the newspaper. But I believe this is all destiny. My purpose for living is to love my family and Marie, and to complete the mission that I have been chosen to do—take the world to the *Beyond the Beyond*.

I sat in this lonely jail cell, depressed that I was wasting time. I needed a pen and paper so I could continue on my journey.

I am going to stop writing about these events for the moment, and go back to where I left off with my life story. I have to do it this way, because this is the way it has been destined to be.

Okay, I had to get back in business. I had to find a way to get the money to do that. This was not an easy task. I already owed a lot of friends and family from my gambling. I had an idea to open an Italian seafood restaurant—not the typical Italian restaurant, but the kind that they have in Little Italy in New York City. There was no such restaurant like that in all of New Jersey. My plan was not only to have the same menu as in Little Italy—fried shrimp, fried calamari, scungilli and shrimp balls, mussels and linguini. The main attraction was the special, unique red gravy that was put on everything. It came in sweet, medium, and hot.

As I'm planning this, it turns out I get lucky, I run into a guy that I knew as a kid. He tells me he is looking to open a restaurant, but he has the same problem as me: no money. He's a fat, lazy slob, but the good thing is he knew a guy that was an accountant, who was looking to invest money in small businesses. Wow! Just what I was looking for. The bad news was for me to get introduced to the accountant, I had to agree to make Nate—the fat, lazy guy— my partner. Even though I knew it was a bad move, knowing how lazy he was, I had no other options at the time.

So I meet the accountant. His name was Richie, but we will call him the Penguin. I gave him this name because he was very short and always wore this long rain coat. When he walked, you would only see his feet moving, and he kind of waddled, so I called him the Penguin. After our meeting, the Penguin agreed to finance the new restaurant. It would be a three-way partnership: me, him, and Nate.

The place I set up was really unique for Jersey. The restaurant clam bar was long and narrow, kind of like the famous Italian clam bar in Little Italy, Vincent's, Umberto's, and Little Charlie's. We had this long counter that seated about twenty-five customers, and then we had a small dining area with about ten tables. Behind the long counter was where all the cooking and frying took place. Right in front of you were the big pots of our famous red sauces—we got the recipe from Little Italy. All the cooking being done in front of you gave the place the atmosphere of being in Little Italy.

The place started out a big success. As I knew from the beginning, my partner, Nate, was lazy. I did all the work. So I made a deal with the Penguin to be bought out for all the work I had done. It turned out to be my biggest score. We agreed that I was entitled to $15,000. Well! As we were making arrangements on how he was going to pay me, I find out that he is a big sports gambler. So I tell him, "You don't have to pay me the $15,000. If you'd like, you could try and win it. Here's the deal I am offering you: I will book all your sports action." I told him there would be no vigs involved (that is the 10% interest the bookies tack on) so he would have an even chance of winning, same as me. And he would pick the teams, and neither one of us would be breaking the law, because if two people are making a personal bet and there is no vig involved, it's legal. He agreed, and we got started. We used whatever the point spreads were in the New York *Daily News*.

Well! I finally found someone who was worse than me. He did nothing but pick losers, week after week. Every week I was winning money; and as soon as I got paid, Angie and I would run to the casinos in Atlantic City. He kept losing for almost two years, week after week, and the sad part was that I had nothing to show for it. At the end of my run with him, he was having a problem paying me for his losses.

Then I found out that he had been running a Ponzi scheme for years, and it all started to fall down. He kept gambling to try and pay all the people that he was taking money from. I had no idea that he was doing that. As I look back, I say to myself if I only knew that he was going to keep losing like he did, I would have just kept putting the money aside to start a new business. The Penguin wound up getting ten years with the Feds for some kind of money fraud. The Penguin's well had finally run dry.

So I have to get back in business. I run into a friend of mine who tells me he just invested in a go-go joint on Paterson Plank Road in East Rutherford, right behind Giant Stadium. When he asks me what I am doing, and I tell him nothing at the moment, he asks if I would be interested in running the food part of the business. I said yes, even though I never really wanted to get into the bar and nightclub scene. Drinking all the time and staying up to all kinds of crazy hours wasn't really my thing. But I said to myself, "*Fuck it, why not? I'm not doing anything.*"

Well! It was just what I thought it would be. I was drinking every night and getting home at all kinds of crazy hours. Every once in a while, I'd have some wild times with the go-go dancers. A lot of the New York Giants football players would come in, being that the practice field was right next to the bar. I eventually became pretty good friends with two linebackers, Brian Kelly and Brad Van Pelt.

But still, after about six months of that lifestyle, I'd had enough. I had to leave the business. It turned out that I went from the frying pan to the fire.

I've got a friend named George. To this day, he is a close friend of mine. Well! He introduces me to cocaine. I had never seen an illegal drug until then in my life, and with my reputation, no one would ever even mention the word drugs in front of me. It was the mid-eighties and that was the height of the popularity of cocaine. I was hearing about all the movie stars and businessmen doing it. When I was told that it was good with sex, well, that convinced me to give it a try.

Oh, my God! Me with my compulsive personality, remember? Okay, that started the coke scene. Here I am at a point where I am depressed over all the money I lost from gambling, so I cop out by starting to use cocaine.

My friend, George, has a small restaurant and bar in the city of Paterson. For the next year, I'm doing coke and hanging out in his restaurant seven days a week. Wow! Was that a fuckin crazy city back then! The city's prosecutor would be up all night doing blow with me and George, and then would go into court the next day to prosecute people that were in court for drug charges. People would have to tell him to wipe the white powder off his nose right in court. I heard that he died a few years later of an overdose.

George's restaurant was downtown Paterson, right next to the courthouse. I couldn't believe the things that went on in that small area, within a five block radius. We had a dentist friend whose office was a block from George's joint. One day, we walked over to visit the dentist. He was working on the mouth of a city judge. He told us that his hands were shaking so much that he needed a line of coke to calm down. That day always stuck in my mind: to see a doctor doing coke as he is working on his patient, a city judge.

Reader, I cannot go on telling my life story in chronological order at this time. It is destiny that I tell my life story before I take you to the *Beyond the Beyond*. But for now I have to write about current events.

So there I was, sitting in the Bergen County Jail in New Jersey waiting to be extradited to New York. A few political friends had reached out to me, offering to have the correctional officers look out for me. I appreciated the courtesy extended to me, but did not accept.

After sitting for fifteen days in the Bergen County Jail, the FBI and the New York City Organized Crime Task Force came to get me and bring me to New York. They were taking me to the infamous Rikers Island Jail—the largest, toughest, and most dangerous jail in the country.

Reader, I *was* going to start talking about me being labeled a member of organized crime, and then I was going to spend some time talking about my experiences doing a four-year sentence in Federal Prison. But as I see it, destiny has told me to stop writing for the moment and talk about the present time—the last two and a half months in Rikers Island.

I was on the bus filled with guys that have just been recently arrested, all somewhat concerned, a lot of the guys nervous and scared, not knowing what to expect, going to the feared Rikers Island Jail. I was mentally preparing myself, putting on my tough guy hat. I was getting the attitude that I would not give up my manhood for anything. I would choose death before I would have any inmate disrespect me. Mentally, I was thinking like I was physically thirty years old, but reality is that I was physically sixty-three!

From the first day that I got to Rikers Island, they spelled my name wrong. They changed the two c's to two l's. So instead of me being Gaccione, I was referred to as Gallione. The first month, every time they called my name for something, they would call me Gallione. I would get so mad and go through this long story about my name being Gaccione, and how they changed it to Gallione and wouldn't correct it. I kept saying that they even took my name from me. After a month of this, a couple of guys I became close with started to laugh when one day they called my name Gallione, and I answered to it. I gave up. I said to myself,

Fuck it, I'm Gallione. Now, for the last couple of months, when my family and friends write to me, they call me Gallione.

After a short time, most of the inmates learned that the New York *Daily News* and *New York Post* were putting me in their newspaper as a member of the mafia. That attracted most of the inmates to me. It is crazy how those shows like *The Godfather*, *Goodfellas*, and *The Sopranos* have this glamor to them, it is just the way it is. Yes, there have been times I have played that roll just for the extra perks.

The toughest part of my incarceration is when I am in the bullpen. Those times are when I am reminded that I am in jail. The bullpen is a holding cell where you have a large number of inmates all jammed together. When I first came in, I had to spend over thirty hours in there before they assigned me to housing.

So far, I am the only guy that refuses to go and lay on the floor. Young and old, eventually after so many hours, hit the floor. With me, it's a mental thing, a self-pride thing, a tough man thing, and an attitude thing. My belief is that the only way you will bring me to the floor is if I pass out, and that almost happened a few times.

I was surprised to see how many fucking crybabies there are in here. When they come to me, I get mad and tell them to be a man and have some pride.

117

One of the reasons I started the book *Beyond the Beyond* by telling my life story is to establish that from as far back as I can remember as a little boy, anywhere I went, anything I have done, I was always in the center of it all. Unintentionally, but always in the limelight. After a while, I noticed that and asked myself, "Why?" I realized there was some kind of purpose and meaning for it to be that way.

As you can see, I am always speaking of destiny.

Well! Story time! About two months before my arrest, during the time I am writing this book, I come across this movie on one of my cable channels. The movie was called *Redemption*. I had no idea what the movie was about, but the name of the movie attracted me. It was about a man called Stanley Tookie-Williams. He was the co-founder of the notorious gang, the Crips. The movie shows him on death row and how he changed his life around in prison. He started writing children's books, mainly trying to help kids stay away from the life of crime—trying to help kids from staying away from all the mistakes that he made. I was so impressed and inspired learning about Tookie Williams. I mention this because it is important for me to say that many people are products of their environment. Here was a man who grew up in the ghetto, grew up amongst street gangs, shootings and murder. When given the chance to expand his mind and use his intellect, he became a Nobel Peace Prize nominee, for writing children's books. I cannot help but think of the movie with Eddie Murphy, *Trading Places,* which supports my theory of you being a product of your environment.

Now after seeing that movie, *Redemption,* and telling so many people about it, two months later, here I am in jail with the Crips in real life. They run the unit that I am in, because half of the fifty inmates in my dormitory are part of the Crips. From what I have seen, they are capable of violence; and from many of the fights that I have seen here, most show that they have a pair of balls. The gang's strength is that if you fight one, you have to fight them all.

When I first got here and saw that, I said to myself, "*I don't stand a chance. The odds are about 99% that one of them is going to disrespect me.*" I know I could never allow that, so my thought was to try my best to get the guy who disrespects me before the gang fucks me up. In my heart and my mind, I choose death over disrespect. As destiny would have it, the respect that I showed not only the gang members but all the inmates in the dorm caught on. Before I knew it, the leaders of the gangs were letting all their guys know that they should go out of their way to show me respect. They also let all the inmates in the dorm know that they should show me extra courtesy.

The thing is that with all the love and respect that I get, I don't take advantage of it. Instead, I give it all back—not just to the gang, but to all the inmates. Funny, but I see some of that rubbing off with the gang members. I have no doubt that it is because of me having the power from the spirit of the *Beyond the Beyond*. At one time or another, every inmate wants to come and sit at the end of my bed and talk, each one having a different motive. Some are looking to talk so they can slowly make a move on a piece of cake, or cookies, or some sugar. Some guys want to hear my opinion on their charges, which ranged from murder, drugs, to purse-snatching thinking I am a wise old man. And some are looking to make a move on me to set them up in business, thinking I'm a rich man. And of course, there are the inmates who are intrigued with the mafia. Based on the image that has been portrayed of me, some hope to hear some exciting mob stories. In each and every case of an inmate coming to talk to me—and I have had well over a hundred private talks with different inmates—I listen to them talk, and I learn so much about their different circumstances in each and every one of their lives. I also pay attention to the environment that they have grown up in. The great majority of them are young—in their late teens or early twenties. They all still have their whole lives ahead of them.

I have no doubt that all of this has been put on my plate because it is all part of destiny, before the story of the *Beyond the Beyond* is told. When the miracle of *Beyond the*

Beyond occurred, I was given the wisdom on how to go about telling it. That is because it is all destined to be this way.

The miracle of *Beyond the Beyond* occurred about two and a half years ago. Now it is July 10, 2010—my girlfriend's birthday—and I was given the wisdom of how to go about telling it. The first step is to tell my life story up to the miracle of the *Beyond the Beyond* and the purpose of telling my life story. The second step is to meet with two of the top intellects of the world. They are Deepak Chopra and Dinish D'Souza. It is destiny that they have been chosen from me. The reason is that they have been blessed and chosen with a high intellect that has brought them to the doorway to the *Beyond the Beyond*.

I know all this as a fact because of what had occurred. None of this could be written about at this point, because I have too much common sense not to go about it in an intelligent way. I have to show I am not delusional or nuts. It will be destiny that will give me the wisdom to reveal the miracle of the *Beyond the Beyond* at the proper time for the world to benefit.

At this time, I have to stop writing. An incredible heat wave has just set in to the jail. As I attempt to write, the sweat drips off my brow and soaks the paper that I'm writing on. The radio said it hit 102 degrees in New York City, which means it is probably 110–120 degrees inside our dormitory, which has fifty inmates in close quarters.

I am getting ready to go to court for a bail hearing. My charge is second degree murder. They say it happened nineteen years ago.

Just to have to write the word "murder" sickens me.

There have been over fifty letters sent to the judge from family and friends, stating that I would never be a risk not to show up for trial. I found out that friends from my hometown and the surrounding towns were planning a fundraising benefit for me. These are up-standing citizens, good people from every walk of life: politicians, law enforcement, big business executives, professional people, doctors, lawyers, teachers, who are all stepping forward on my behalf. My heart was touched when I heard this, but I could not accept.

The day I had to go to court for my bail hearing, it was 120 degrees on the bus. I truly believed I was going to get a stroke. I knew it would not happen only because I know that it is destiny for me to finish this book.

When I walked into the courtroom with my hands in handcuffs, I couldn't look into the seats. Every single one was filled with my family and friends. I knew that if I saw my loved ones it would bring me to tears.

For the second time, the judge has not ruled on giving me bail or not. He has postponed the hearing for another two and a half months, claiming that he has not had time to review the grand jury minutes on my indictment. On the way back from court to Rikers Island Jail, about half of the thirty guys on the bus almost passed out from the heat. It had to have hit 120 degrees on the bus.

When I got back to my dorm, I had no time to be depressed that I had to wait another two and a half months for the opportunity to try and get bail. I just counted every minute of the next three day's incredible heat wave, waiting for it to end. My entire goal was to live through this, and then I can mentally regroup to do the things that I am destined to do.

I have to write my lawyer and let him know how unhappy I am with him. I also have to write the judge—there is so much that needs to be said, but until the weather breaks and this incredible heat wave ends, I cannot think clearly. All I do know is that if the leaders of the Crips didn't show me the respect that they have been showing me, I think I would have had a stroke. There are two fans in our dorm, and the Crips control them. They make sure that one of those fans directly blows on me. As mentally strong as I know that I am, I also believe my health would be in serious danger without that fan. It is part of destiny that the Crips take care of me, the same way that it is destiny for the completion of the *Beyond the Beyond* to be written.

In the corner of my dormitory, there are about ten or twelve inmates that meet every morning and every evening to pray and have a Bible meeting. They are all Christians. I don't attend, although I do encourage the ones that go. They've been having these prayer meetings since I have been here. A couple of days ago, I was invited by the inmate who runs these services to be a guest speaker. It was last night that I attended their services. I started to speak with the words, "Where two or more gather in his name, there will he be." These words will be relevant later in the book.

My message to the inmates which I received from *Beyond the Beyond* was that from the day that we are born to our final day alive, our destinies has already been mapped out by the Almighty, but only *He* knows what that is. The thing that we have to be aware of at all times is that we can influence our destinies every day, good or bad, by our actions. My message to you, reader, is that although your destiny has already been decided, you can help to influence where it is going by the effort you put into it each and every day.

I tell you in truth, this is one of the most important messages that you can receive for your life. Being positive will *always* defeat being negative. These messages are not from me—they come from the *Beyond the Beyond*.

ᴄᎶᎧ *Chapter Seven* ᎣᎯ

A bout two weeks have passed since I wrote my last words. It has been so hot that I could barely function. This summer in New York City has broken every record for high temperatures since they have started recording the weather.

My belief is so strong that I should not waste this time thinking about how I am locked up. Instead, I need to spend it on my writing. I believe that this is the most important journey of my life.

After I write about six or seven handwritten scribbled pages, I mail them to my sister-in-law, Donna Marie, so she can correct my spelling and then get my work typed up. She then mails the typed pages back to me. How ironic that I have her doing this for me, when seven years ago, I had a tremendous hatred for her. Seven years ago my younger brother, Mark, came up from Florida to live with me. Since he was young, he had a drinking problem. That always bothered me, knowing what a great human being he was. He had a lot of talent that went to waste.

Well! The first week he's in town from Florida, he meets up with Donna Marie in a bar. They knew each other from when they were kids. It turns out she's snorting heroin and he's doing cocaine and drinking. Within months, my brother was so fucked-up that I had to ask him to leave my house. I wanted to kill myself for having to do that. I love him so much, but I had no other choice. I blamed it all on Donna Marie for corrupting him.

Then he comes to me and says that she is pregnant. She was in her late forties and never had a child. My advice to him was to encourage her to have an abortion since I knew that they were both fucked-up. I remember her coming to me and saying, "I want to be a mother so bad, I'm going to straighten my life out and take care of my child."

I opened my heart to her and said, "I'll try in every way to help you, if you want to help yourself."

As destiny had it, she gave birth to a great adorable living soul—a beautiful little girl—and they made me her godfather. Donna Marie has been off dope since June 27, 2003. She first started going to a drug program in the North Jersey area. She got pregnant in October 2003 and gave birth on July 5, 2004. I know no greater or prouder mother than her.

I now love her. I am proud to call her my sister-in-law. The odds were so heavily against her—and she continues to beat those odds, one day at a time. All this her destiny—the same way she is destined to be part of a book that will have such a great purpose.

Back to my life story. I have to tell this story all the way up to the miracle of the *Beyond the Beyond*. So from where I left off, I am gambling, partying, and doing coke. During this time, I meet this tough mobster. He was coming to collect a gambling debt that I had with a bookie. He was a big, strong man with a face that only a mother could love. When Johnny Moose looked at someone, most people would get scared to death. The way it turned out, we had a standoff as far as balls were concerned. As it turns out, we eventually become friends.

About a year later, he comes to my house late at night and asks me for a favor. He wants me to go with him and his brother to remove a garbage can that was filled with an accelerant that was in a racquetball club. He was trying to burn the place down, but the sprinkler system went off and put the fire out. He wanted me to go back with him to get rid of the garbage can that had the gasoline in it.

Stupid me, I go back with him and his brother to go get the garbage can. After we take it out of the building, we put it in the back seat of his car. At 3:00 a.m., we leave the shopping mall where the racquetball club was located. As we're getting ready to get on the highway, a patrol car for the city of Paramus stops us. They were questioning us on what we were doing in the mall area at 3:00 in the morning.

We almost got away when I started to tell the police officer that just two months earlier, I was one of the guest speakers at a testimonial dinner for the mayor of Paramus.

He was my old high school football coach and I was asked to speak at the dinner. The cop was just about ready to let us go until he put his flashlight into the garbage can on the seat. We were arrested, and the next day when the newspapers came out—because my friend was labeled a member of the mafia—they accused me of being an associate of the mob. That was the start of people looking at me like I was a mobster.

As it turned out, I copped to some low level charge. I couldn't even tell you exactly what the charge was—I didn't care. I knew I wasn't going to get in any more trouble, so it didn't matter to me. I got a year of probation for that.

Now! Not too long after that happened, a friend of my father came to me, asking me if I could help him collect money that was owed to him for the sale of his bar. This was the start of people coming to me with different problems, thinking I was in the mafia. I got my father's friend all the money that was owed to him for the sale of the bar. It turns out that I became good friends with the young man who bought the bar.

After about a year later, my friend Louie Aurrechio offered me an opportunity to take over a business he owned in the Meadowlands. It was a gourmet deli and restaurant with a mini-grocery attached. It was in the beautiful Harmon Cove Towers in Secaucus, New Jersey, which is in the heart of the Meadowlands. This place was beautiful! He told me he had put a million dollars into setting this business up; and from what it looked like, I believed him. He told me that the people that he had running the business are doing a bad job and he is losing money. He offered me the opportunity to just take the place over. I did not have to give him a dime. All I had to do was to pay the bills and give him a small monthly payment to buy the place from him.

I went to my two brothers and brought them in as partners. All our children would come in from time to time to help out. This was so important to me because it was an opportunity for me to try and bond more with my children. My father was one of the main reasons we really improved the business. My father had become pretty well-known in our area for his Italian cooking. He had these special Italian recipes that were his own creations. In fact, a close friend of my father's owned a plumbing company. He asked my father if he would teach him to cook and give him all of his recipes. My father did so, and the friend opened up one of the most famous Italian restaurants in North Jersey. Francesco's Restaurant was located in Clifton and Passaic, New Jersey. The table I would always sit at was half in one town and half in the other town.

In the Towers where the deli-restaurant that I took over was located, there were about eight hundred apartments. Many of the top New York executives had an apartment there. It was just ten minutes from Manhattan. There were also a lot of the pro-sport athletes that lived there—players from the Yankees, Mets, Nets, Jets, Knicks, and Giants. Many of the stars would come into our place. I remember one time, Bill Cartwright, who was playing center for the New York Knicks, came into the deli. My aunt was so excited to see a man that big. He was seven feet four inches tall. As she began to ask him a question about basketball, he was extremely rude to her. When I saw that my aunt started to cry, I got really mad and started to verbally abuse him, challenging him to a fight. When he didn't take me up on the offer, I told him to get out and don't come back. From time to time, when I think back to the incident, I ask myself how I could have hit him. I would have needed a stepstool he was so big.

During the year and a half that I am trying to get the business to be a success, my friend Louis is starting to get his name in the newspaper. The papers were calling him a rising star in the Genovese crime family. That never deterred me from remaining his friend. I never did anything illegal with him or knew any illegal activity that he was involved with.

In the meantime, he introduces me to these three guys. They're all brothers-in-law, and they live with their families in the towers. So they would often come in to the gourmet deli. After getting to know them for a short while, I find out they are selling cocaine. They were selling in large amounts, but they would do me and my friend, George, a favor and sell us just a couple of eight-balls. An eight-ball is three and one-half grams. Sometimes, they wouldn't even charge me.

They were doing so well that they moved into these three beautiful homes that they had built. The houses were located in a cul-de-sac with about eight houses in a rich town in North Jersey. So, my friend George and I would start going to their new homes to pick up our shit. We were actually a nuisance to them since they were doing such big business and were so busy. The way it turned out was they got busted and George and I got arrested with fifty other people. They were selling cocaine in one, two, and three kilos to fifty different people. These people were just all people who got hooked on cocaine, and then started selling it. Cocaine was so popular back then that all of them were becoming big dealers overnight. They were all making a lot of money. When the DEA made the bust, they said, "The business was so big that they were openly running their drug businesses like it was legal, as if they had a license."

Almost every one of the fifty defendants pled guilty. Between the surveillance and the phone taps, the DEA had everyone dead in the water. There were only three guys that went to trial, along with me and George. Not only were George and I not drug dealers, but we only bought a small amount for ourselves. The problem was that when the jury heard fifty different people calling saying, "Give me one or give me two or three," there was no way to know if they were referring to kilos or ounces. The DEA was able to prove that for everyone, so when the jury heard the phone tapes of George and I, they just assumed we were talking about kilos and ounces, when we were talking about grams.

I remember seeing the US Assistant Attorney in the men's room during the trial, and him saying to me, "Doc, I know you're not a drug dealer. If you give me information on illegal activity of Louis Aurecchio, we'll drop your charges." Now, I made it a point to never want to know any of my street friend's business. If for some reason I would have accidentally known something, I would never be a rat—it's just not what I am.

Near the end of the trial, as bizarre as it might sound, one of the jurors fell in love with George. The way it turned out, the jury convicted me and the other two defendants, and there was a hung jury on George; it was eleven to one to convict him.

The day I went for sentencing, I was so naive. I thought I was going to get a two-year sentence, and that's only because I felt I was going to get punished for going to trial. The feds give you extra time when you take your case to trial and lose compared to if you would have pled guilty and saved the government time and money. I innocently thought that I wouldn't get extra time because I knew I was no drug dealer. A couple of days before the sentencing, I get this strong premonition to write a letter to the judge. The day of sentencing, as I'm standing before the judge, he says, "I've just read your letter, and I feel it is the most candid letter I have ever read."

In the meantime, I am nervously asking myself, *"What does candid mean?"*

Then the judge says, "I'm going to do something unprecedented. I'm going to cut your sentence in half. I've never done this before." He then said, "From eight years, I am changing your sentence to four years!"

I remember my knees buckling from the thought that I could have gotten eight years for cocaine. Later, after I thought about it, I was so grateful that at the last minute I'd had a premonition to write the letter to the judge. The letter was saying how strong I was against drugs and then telling how I got caught up in doing drugs. Then I explain that I was no drug dealer. The judge gave me a two-month stay before I had to self-surrender. During this time, one of my close uncles passed away. It was the first time I was present to see someone take his last breath. At that very moment that I saw him take his last breath, I saw this flash of light leave his body. I dismissed it from my mind, thinking it was just part of an imagination. I've never told a single person this until now, as I write it down.

The time had come for me to self-surrender. I had the attitude that I was happy to do the time. I felt I needed the time to get my head together. I said to myself, *"I won't waste one minute of the time I have to serve! I will work on myself physically, mentally, and spiritually. Somehow, I don't know how, I'll even come up with an idea to make money in there."*

Still, this was the lowest point of my life, going to federal prison for four years. My positive attitude was so strong that being so positive even got my attention. I started to reflect back on my first memories—how, from the time I was a little kid up until then, I had never allowed a negative thought to overcome my positive attitude.

So there I was, on a little prop airplane flying to upstate New York to Lake Placid. That is where the federal correctional institution, called Raybrook FCI, was located. It was the Olympic village where the athletes lived for the 1980 Winter Olympic Games that the US hosted. After the games were over, the feds turned it into a correctional facility. It was so beautiful for an FCI that I was told that the government used it as a showplace for the rest of the world to see our federal correctional facilities.

After I landed at this tiny airport, I called a taxi cab to drive me for a five-minute ride to get to Raybrook FCI. After spending about two hours in the processing building, the correctional officer told me to go outside and walk over to the building where I was assigned to be housed. I'll never forget the impression I had when I walked outside and saw these beautiful manicured lawns with these beautiful flower beds of all different colors. It looked like I was on a college campus.

It was the middle of August when I arrived. As I was walking along this asphalt walkway, there were inmates riding bikes. Then as I continued to walk towards my building, I saw inmates passing by me on roller-blades. As my mouth hung wide open with confusion, here came inmates, jogging along in different colored designer jogging suits. At this point, I stopped walking and said to myself, *"Am I in the right place? Did I accidentally come to a country club?"*

After I arrived at my building, the officer assigned me to my cell, which was actually a small room with a sink, toilet, little table, and double bunks. When I got settled from making up my bed and arranging my clothes, I walked over to the main area of the dorm. That is where they had the TVs, telephone, and a lounge area. It was while I was walking towards that area when I meet my first fellow inmate. Johnny Serubo was in his late twenties when I met him. He was a small, cocky, smart, good-looking manipulator. He was a good salesman—maybe that's because he was a partner with his father in a Cadillac dealership in the city of Philadelphia. Most people in the Philly area had heard of Serubo Cadillac.

I saw right away that this kid was a good friend to have, the way he maneuvered around the prison. The first thing this guy did for me was to get me a job in the weightlifting gym. Every inmate in the correctional institute had to have a job; that was mandatory. What a score that was for me to be able to get that job! It was the hardest job in the whole place to get. All you had to do is put the dumbbells or plates back on the racks, once in a while.

So this job gave me the opportunity to work out whenever I wanted and for however long I wanted. This was important to me, because it was one of the goals that I set for myself. I knew the importance of getting back my good build. I knew that I had the knowledge to turn that into an advantage in life. I'm also a strong believer that the mind works at an optimal level when the body is working at an optimal level. By the same token, the body cannot work at an optimal level if the mind is not at an optimal level.

This is one of my strongest beliefs, so I knew I had to use this principal for myself to take advantage of my incarceration. Within the first couple of months that I was there, muscles started popping out all over me. The inmates could not believe their eyes over my transformation in such a short time. I guess that I was proof that muscles have memories.

As the months went by, my physique continued to take form. The inmates were also in awe of the exceptional strength that came to me in just a short time. Soon, I became the strongest inmate in the entire prison. That's a big deal in the joint—it is some kind of macho shit. Because of that, I became one of the most popular and talked-about inmates in the joint. It got to a point where even the correctional officers and administrators started to take a special notice of me.

No one could believe the positive attitude that I displayed. When I would comment that I was happy to be there, I was laughed at and joked about in a respectful way. That was something that was hard to believe—not just for the inmates, but also for the administrators. You never heard a prisoner saying he was happy to be in jail, but I knew that this was the perfect place for me to get myself back on track physically, mentally, and spiritually. So as the months were starting to pass by, I continued to get bigger, stronger, and mentally in the right frame of mind. I was starting to get back my business creativity. I just knew that with my positive attitude and with me starting to get my mind right, somehow I would come up with a business idea in here to make money. I had no idea how, but I just knew I would do it.

In the meantime, Johnny Serubo and I became close friends. I also became close friends with Serubo's roommate, Peter LaMonie. He was a boss in the Boston mob. So Serubo, with me and LaMonie as close friends, walked around the compound in a confident way. I didn't mind, because he always took care of me. Anything I wanted, he would maneuver to get—especially food. He made sure I ate like a king. He knew what an incredible appetite I had, especially now that I started serious weight training.

So at nighttime, Peter, Serubo and I would sit around and bullshit as we were eating like kings. Serubo made sure Pete and I had anything we wanted. It was like a scene from a movie about the mob. I remember one night when we were shooting the breeze, Serubo was telling a story about how he and his father had opened one of the first video rental stores in Philly. He said he hired one of the top porn stars of the day to sign autographs of her picture at his grand opening. He then told us how at the end of the day, he took her and her girlfriend to a coke-snorting orgy all night long. That interested me because she was my favorite porn star.

The story LaMonie told that night, I cannot write about, even though he's long dead. I heard he died of cancer at the early age of forty-two. Even if I can't tell the story, I'll say this: I cannot believe he told Serubo and me.

That night, I remember telling them a story about when I first got arrested and spent six months in the Metropolitan Correctional Center in Manhattan waiting to get bail. I remember two of the five mafia families' bosses being there with me: John Gotti and Junior Persico. Well! In the six months waiting to get bail, I really got myself in physical shape working out with mop brooms and water buckets. A couple of weeks before I got released from the MCC, there was this female correctional officer (C.O.) that got put on our floor. She was a knock-out! She had a great figure and looked like Jennifer Lopez, one of my favorites. Well! I don't know if it was my imagination or not, but I felt like she was giving me sexual advances. It was hard for me to believe, since I was far from good-looking and she was so hot, but I was sure she was coming on to me.

One night, a few days before I was getting ready to get out on bail, this C.O. locks down every tier on the floor, and then does my tier. She locks down every room but mine. That was the first night that I did not have a cellmate—he had just left the day before. Well! When she entered my room, I was hot, horny, excited, and nervous at the same time. She made an advance at me. She wanted to have sex in my bunk in my room. Although I thought I'd picked up those vibrations for the last week, I still could not believe that I was right. As great as the temptation was, I turned her down in a nice way. I was scared. I was paranoid that I was being set up. I already knew that the FBI believed that I had information about mafia friends of mine. I felt they would try and set me up with a federal corrections officer on a rape charge so they could try and get me to give information they assumed I had. She was so attractive that I was sick at the thought of not being able to take advantage of the opportunity, but it was something I couldn't risk. So, that's the story I told Serubo and LaMonie.

A couple of months after I told that story, one evening about 6:30 Serubo, LaMonie, and I, along with a couple of other friends, were outside sitting on a park bench. A bus pulled up with a bunch of inmates coming from MCC in New York City. It turned out that we knew one of the guys who came in on the bus. As we started to bullshit with him, he started to tell a story how there was this beautiful correctional officer at the MCC that he was having sex with. It turned out that it was the same C.O. that I told the story about. It turned out that it wasn't my big arms that turned her on, but her thinking I was in the mafia. The moral of the story is that I could have had sex with her, but better safe than sorry.

When winter came in Raybrook, everyone knew it. When you had a runny nose, it would freeze from it being so cold. Raybrook was only a few miles from the Canadian border. At any given time in the winter, temperatures could drop as low as 10–20 degrees below zero. By the time the heart of winter came, I was into long, grueling workouts. To psych myself up before my workouts in the winter, I would go out and walk from my building to the gym in my shorts. By the time I arrived at the gym, my legs were so cold that I couldn't feel them; but within minutes, they would thaw out. Inmates and the administration alike thought I was fuckin' nuts, but whatever would prepare me for a three-hour-forty-five-minute workout, I would do.

After spending a year at Raybrook and really getting into my self-improvement program, physically, mentally, and spiritually, I was notified that I was being moved to another correctional institute. I was heartbroken when I got the news. I had become the most popular, well-liked, and respected inmate in the joint, and now I had to leave. I had a special relationship with the black groups, the Hispanic groups, the white groups and, of course, the Italian groups. I guess that's one of the reasons I stuck out: I was able to relate to everyone.

It was hard to keep my positive attitude over the move. Here I was, so comfortable doing my time, and now I had to move to another prison. I couldn't imagine that I could have it as good in another joint as I did at Raybrook. The one optimistic thing I had to look forward to was that Johnny Serubo's father was at the new joint that I was being transferred to. That was the Federal Correctional Institute of Danbury, Connecticut. My other close friend, Peter LaMonie, had given me the names of a few of his Boston mafia friends who were at Danbury. The custom with the Italians is that when you go to a new joint and mention a name to the guys that are there, they go out of their way to help set you up.

Well! To my surprise, the next two years at the FCI of Danbury were so incredible that I felt I had to write about it. The first person I looked up when I arrived at Danbury was Johnny Serubo's father. His name was Pete, the same as my buddy LaMonie's name. Johnny had asked me to look out for his father, which I was happy to do. I also had a motive that knowing he was a big businessman on the street.

I had hoped if we got close, I might have a business opportunity become available for me.

The first and most important thing Pete Serubo did for me as soon as I arrived was to get me the best job in the prison. It was a job he had, and he finagled for me to be his assistant. The job was to run the diet line. That was to serve food to inmates that were diabetics or on low-sodium diets. The job took us ten minutes to do, twice a day, and all the rest of the day was ours. This was even a better score than my job at the gym at Raybrook, because I had the complete perks of the chow hall. And as I will tell you, that was big.

I was immediately able to start spending my entire afternoon in the gym, weight training. My training was becoming so vigorous and intense that the toughest twenty or twenty-five-year-old guys at the joint could not last training with me over a week or two. After about three months of being there, I found out that the recreation department had weightlifting teams from the outside come to the prison to compete with us. They would give these beautiful, big trophies to the winners of each lift. At the age of forty, I worked my bench press back up to 550 pounds. Every time they had the competition, I won the first place trophies. After a while, I had won so many trophies that I started to change the name plate on the trophies, and award them to the guys who were able to last for a while when training with me.

One of my favorite pastimes, other than my training, was to talk to different inmates who were not my friends. In federal prison, unlike most state prisons, there are an exceptional number of highly intelligent inmates. As it turns out, most of them are too smart for their own good. There are people from every walk of life: doctors, lawyers, politicians, big business men, even different religious leaders. There are also big-time drug dealers and smugglers, and every type of intelligent criminal that you could think of. I would enjoy talking to all of them. When a jerk-off would come around me telling me how many people he killed, I would blow him off. I couldn't waste my time with assholes. But all the rest, I would enjoy talking to. People have always interested me— how they think, how they feel, how they react. This is how I have always learned—from other people.

There was this one incident that happened with one of my young workout partners that still makes me laugh. This guy was about twenty-five years old. He was a Hells Angel. The funny thing about all the Hells Angels motorcycle gang members that I met during my time in prison is that there wasn't one that was 100% physically intact. They either had arms, legs, hands, ears, eyes, or fingers missing from their bike riding. This one Hells Angel who was working out with me for a few weeks had an artificial leg that resulted from a motorcycle accident. Well! One day he was late for the start of our workout, and the smoke was starting to come out of my ears. I didn't approve of workout partners showing up late for a workout. As I was just getting ready to start my workout without him, he showed up, walking into the gym on crutches. I asked him, "What the fuck happened?"

He replied, "I'm sorry I'm late, but I had to go in front of the disciplinary board for an incident I had a few weeks ago. The sentence they gave me was thirty days in the box. But then they gave me an option: I could give them my leg for thirty days to replace my sentence. I told them, Fuck it, take the leg."

I busted out laughing! I found it so funny that they took his leg for disciplinary reasons.

I had mentioned when I was getting ready to start my prison sentence that I was going to take advantage of the time, and somehow come up with an idea to make money. Well! One day as I am in the middle of a workout, a thought comes to me. It was the first time I became aware of the importance of my rest intervals between the sets of my exercises. This is when I invented the *Doc Watch*, a bodybuilding stopwatch that would put you on a high-tech level of weight training. The Doc Watch fulfills one of the most important, but often overlooked, aspects of the bodybuilding/weight training workout: the rest interval. It has been determined through years of study and experience, at the professional level, that the most important part of muscle development is the rest period. Most bodybuilders and people who train think of this in terms of days and muscle groups, but they miss the obvious: the in-between-set rest period. It is during this period that we must precisely determine and monitor the recuperation of strength.

It's important to pace yourself properly through a workout. If you attempt to train too quickly, you risk premature muscular failure before you've worked the muscles enough. Also, you may have a tendency to lose your form and not execute each movement correctly. However, training too slowly is not good. If you take five minutes between each set, your heart rate slows down, you lose your pump, your muscles get cold, and your level of intensity drops to nothing! During the first minute after a weight training exercise, you recover 72% of your strength. By three minutes, you have recovered all that you're going to recover without extended rest. Remember, the point of weight training is to stimulate and fatigue the maximum amount of muscle fiber possible. This process only happens when the body is forced to recruit additional muscle fiber to replace that which is already fatigued. So you do not want to allow your muscles to recover too much between sets—just enough to continue your workout and keep forcing the body to innervate more and more muscle tissue.

There is one other factor to consider. Physiologists have long noted the link between maximal muscle strength and muscle endurance. Simply put, the stronger you are, the more times you can lift a sub-maximal amount of weight. This means that the more you press yourself to develop *muscular* endurance, as opposed to cardiovascular endurance, the stronger you become! So, maintaining a regular pace in your training actually leads to an increase in overall strength.

With the Doc Watch, you could set the mode button for whatever rest time you desired, and then a buzzer would go off telling you that you were ready for your next set. I could elaborate much more on the features of the watch, but I am not going to. The bottom line about my idea is that it was sound and had great validity. This I immediately knew with my experience and background in physical culture and weight training. As important as the truth of the concept is, I knew the marketing potential of this invention. I've heard from marketing sources that they could care less if an item works; their only interest is in the possible sales potential it would have.

Now, at this time, I was greatly excited for the introduction of my new concept. I was so optimistic that the Doc Watch was going to be a big financial success. I knew it was never done before. I knew the need and benefits for it and I was positive with my God-given vision that if it was marketed correctly, the Doc Watch would be a phenomenal financial success. So the last final year of my sentence, I anxiously waited to be released to work on my ideas and concept to become a reality. I knew I was going to make money from my ideas just like I told myself.

More important to me than the money I anticipated making was my excitement at the thought of making my children proud of me. After the embarrassment of going to prison—on a drug charge, no less—the thought of coming up with an idea that could have such an influence on bodybuilding and weight-training really made me proud. Making my children proud of me was so much more important than financial success.

In the meantime, things are really going better than just good as I'm doing my time. On a Sunday afternoon in the chow hall, we would have a couple of Italian guys cooking Italian food, a couple of black guys making some soul food, and a couple of Hispanic guys cooking some Hispanic food. Then we would all share our different ethnic foods with each other. The entire prison would be locked down for the main count, and here we would be in the chow hall, having a feast. The funny thing about that was the correctional officers who were in charge of the mess hall would ask us for some food. The other guys would tell them, "Hold on. If there's some left over, we'll give you some." I used to have to hold my dick, not to piss in my pants, I found that so funny.

All the C.O.s had to do is say, "Look, jerks. Give us some food first or we'll put you in the hole." But we had them so brainwashed that they never even thought that way. We would sit around and have a feast with food as good as anything from a restaurant. It looked like one of those mob scenes in the movies.

I was having my way around that prison in a way that even I could not believe. I was so popular and well-liked by the staff in the different departments of the prison. Whenever they had a problem with a different department, they would come to me to take care of it. The heads of the different departments would have fights among themselves, so when they needed a favor from another department, they would come to me to take care of it.

I remember one time I wanted to see a heavyweight championship fight that was being shown on closed-circuit TV. I went to the recreation department and talked them into getting the closed-circuit telecast of the Mike Tyson/Michael Spinks fight. I will never forget how badly I wanted to see that fight! And thanks to my salesmanship, the entire prison saw that fight at a cost of $10,000 to the prison.

Now! I was getting short—when you're "short" it means you only have a few months left before you'll be released. I was walking around the joint, happy-go-lucky, like it's my hometown. All of a sudden, one night at dinnertime in the chow hall, this nasty inmate from Washington, DC, throws his dish of food at me because he didn't like it. Well! I beat the shit out of that mother-fucker, and the C.O.s turned their heads like they didn't see anything.

That night it was raining, so there was no one on the compound grounds when I left the mess hall. After I had walked about twenty yards, I had three inmates come around me. They were all wearing federal-issued raincoats. One of them was the guy I fucked up in the chow hall, and the other two were his friends. They all had both their hands in their pockets. I was sure they all had shanks, and I knew they were going to use them.

I knew the only chance I had of not getting killed was to not act scared and to use psychology on them. I turned the tables. I became the aggressor, telling the guy I had the beef with that I was going to kill him by snapping his head off. I said that no matter what his friends were going to do to me, I was going to snap his head off instantly.

I knew they were getting scared at that point, because they knew how strong I was. I kept talking shit to them as I was slowly walking to my dorm. It turned out they never made their move. I know they were capable to do what they set out to do, and it was only me and how I fucked with their heads that got me through that situation.

When I got back to my dorm, I went to a couple of friends who had metal letter openers that they used as shanks. The next day, I got some friends I knew I could count on, and we went out onto the compound grounds. We were ready for a confrontation, but it never happened. For a week, I had my guard up whenever I was working out in the gym. That was the easiest place to kill someone by smashing their head with the plates and dumbbells. So as incredible of a time that I had serving a federal prison sentence at both joints that I was at, the bottom line is that I was in prison. When you're in prison, at any given time, you could be in a life or death situation.

Just as I started to count down my last thirty days, a bus pulls up with new inmates. To my surprise, one of those inmates was my friend Louis Aurrechio. He told me the Feds convicted him to a twelve year sentence for tax evasion. I remember him bragging, saying they gave him more time for tax evasion than Al Capone. The Feds had really wanted his ass for years. There would be times I would go out to eat with him, and federal agents would have him under surveillance. Many times, he would actually pull his pants down and moon them. I would always tell him that he was nuts, so why aggravate them? They would only work extra-hard to get you arrested.

In the four weeks that we were in Danbury together, he made a big splash. He came into the joint really cocky and confident. The year before his arrest, he was getting all kinds of publicity in the newspapers. They kept calling him "a rising star in the Genovese crime family." That was probably because he was the number one suspect for the murder of Johnny Digilio, who was the most powerful and influential member of the Genovese family in North Jersey.

When I was getting ready to get out, Louie made arrangements for his close friend, John Mamone, to come pick me up. I had met Mamone a couple of times on the street at one of Aurrechio's businesses. John Mamone had a big trucking company and was also a builder of new homes. I was so happy he was going to pick me up, because I had confidence that I would get him to invest in the Doc Watch.

Sure enough, over the course of the two hour ride from Danbury, Connecticut, to my brother's house in Nutley, New Jersey, I had sold him on investing and becoming my partner. So within the first two hours that I was released, I made the money that I had said I would make the whole time I was incarcerated.

ᥫ᭡ *Chapter Eight* ᥫ᭡

It is time for me to stop writing my story for the moment and go back to Rikers Island, where I am. The last I spoke of me being at Rikers Island was about three months ago. Back then, I wrote about the record-breaking heat temperatures, and the judge's ruling to keep putting off his decision on giving me bail.

At this time, I have been here for six months. My lawyer has been telling me for the last six months that I shouldn't count on getting bail, because this judge does not give bail for murder cases.

Well! Last week, I went for a bail hearing. About one week before the hearing, I got this strong premonition to write the judge a letter. It was the same type of premonition I had gotten when I wrote the federal judge before my sentence—the one that led to me being incarcerated for four years instead of eight.

The day of my court hearing, I was denied bail again. I turned to my lawyer and told him to ask the judge if he had read my letter. The judge responded, "No, I didn't, but I'll read it right now on the bench." The whole courtroom was filled with family and friends, all anxiously waiting as the court clerk went into my files to get my letter. There was great anticipation as everyone tried to read the expression on the judge's face as he read the letter.

When he was through reading the letter, as he was taking off his reading glasses, he looked straight into my eyes and replied, "I've had a change of heart, and I'm going to give you bail." The bail he set was $1,000,000.00.

At this time, I am waiting to see if that amount of bail could be raised by my family and friends for my release.

In the meantime, I would like to reflect back on the last three months that I have spent here. I haven't talked about that time yet.

To my surprise, I have done something that I cannot even believe I was able to do. When I came in here six months ago, after my arrest, I was not in good health. About three weeks before my arrest, I was rushed to the emergency room four times in one week. Once was for dizzy spells, and three times were for arthritis and bursitis attacks to my shoulder. The pain was so bad that I went to the hospital to beg for a needle to kill the pain. Physically, I looked like a man who had never had the physique that I once had.

Well! At the age of sixty-three, in poor health, I decided I was going to get back in shape and improve my health. Something came over me—some knowledge of the importance of being in good health for the journey with my book, *Beyond the Beyond*.

Taking advantage of my knowledge in physical fitness, I started out with a five-minute workout. That was the first exercise workout that I had done in the past twenty years. Through those twenty years of atrophy, at least 90% of my muscle mass and muscle tone was lost. As I am writing this, it's been five and a half months since my first five-minute workout. Now, I have worked my training sessions up to an hour and one-half.

The result I have received for my efforts is something that amazes me at this stage of my life. The inmates in my dormitory cannot believe their eyes. The majority of them are all young, and they exercise somewhat, but they've never seen such incredible gains and physical improvement in such a short period of time. At this time, it's hard for anyone to miss my new physique, particularly because of my age.

Personally, I am very happy for the health benefits that I have achieved, but I am also happy for having become an example—a role model—for many of these young men, to be an example of what hard work and discipline can accomplish. I have started to share the wisdom I have received from *Beyond the Beyond* with these young men. I start by letting them be aware of the importance of having a goal and direction in their lives. Most of them don't even have an idea about where they are going or what they want to be.

The most important thing that I noticed in my six months living among the youth of the inner city is their fuckin music. One of the strongest influences in the youth of the country is music. What I have noticed here is sickening, especially with the rap music. It talks about shooting, killing, and violence. These young inmates walk around this dorm with their radios, constantly rapping about all this violence and drive-by-shooting shit. They know every word of these fuckin poisonous songs by heart.

Also, I still can't get used seeing all these inmates who are interested in watching *cartoons* on the TV. These are young men—fathers of one, two, three, and sometimes even four children—who have the mentality of children themselves.

There is this one inmate who calls himself Killer. He is a member of the Crips. I developed a special liking for him. He just turned twenty-one while spending the last six months with me at Rikers Island. Here's a young man with normal intelligence, but only a fourth-grade education. This kid was some ball-buster, but in a respectful way. I gave him the name Scutch. He was so witty with these wise-ass remarks, but always done in a respectful way. There was something special about him that always made me laugh. He had such wittiness in him that it just showed his underdevelopment in his education. He won my heart when, after being in the dorm only a couple of days, I noticed him fighting three guys at one time. I didn't know how to react, seeing him get roughed up. I was just getting ready to step in when the action came to a complete stop. It turned out that he was going through his initiation to get into the Crips gang. I guess it was a wise choice that I did not interfere with their ceremony.

I will just take the time to point out one other inmate named Kip Purdie. The Crips gave him the nickname Man-Child. He is a forty-five year old, middle-aged black guy. He's a good looking guy with a good build who exercises and keeps himself in good shape. I started to get to know him when he offered to take over bringing me special foods from the kitchen. This was something that I had another inmate doing, but that inmate was leaving soon. When Man-Child saw how I was taking care of the other inmate who was feeding me the extras, he made his move right away to start taking care of me. So I put him on my payroll, and he was in charge of my food, toilet paper, and ice. He was the worst food lugger I've ever had, but it was worth it just to have him as a friend. He was the only inmate that I've found who I can have an intelligent conversation with. He carries himself as a *respectful* gentleman, and that is the most important thing to me.

He's mentioned to me a few times that he's a really good pickpocket; but judging by the amount of toilet paper that he steals us, I have to question how good of a pickpocket he is. What I do not question is my opinion of his ability to be a successful member of society. He's told me that he's been in and out of jail since he was a kid. I strongly believe—in fact, I know this for truth, since meeting him—that he is going to get his life together and take advantage of his God-given ability and intelligence. I know this because the spirit of the *Beyond the Beyond* has touched him through me.

As I look back on the last six months that I have spent in Rikers Island Jail, I see I have left my mark. This has been confirmed by the correctional officers, administrators, and inmates. I have become the most talked about and respected inmate on the island. Maybe it's because I was put in the worst building in the worst dormitory. All the correctional officers hated to work that dorm; we had the worst reputation. Every bad, disrespectful, violent thing took place in our dormitory. When I first came into the dorm, I was portrayed as this big member of the mafia because of articles that were in the New York newspapers. The way I now see it, that's what gave me a spotlight, and it's never left. After seeing in a short time all the respect that was being showed to me from inmates and C.O's alike, I attributed that to the way I carried myself.

When I started to see the influence I was having on some of the young inmates, I started to sponsor different activities. One of the activities is the daily lottery pick-it number. Since I'm from New Jersey, I use the New Jersey Pick 3 Lottery results each day. The way I do it is each inmate uses the last three numbers of the booking case number on his ID card. Every day, I post the winning New Jersey Pick 3 number on our bulletin board. I personally pay the winners. The payout is $4.00 worth of commissary food or candy for a box hit, and $20.00 for a straight hit.

After seeing that this activity was overwhelmingly appreciated, I decided to have a football pool since it was football season. I would have every inmate participate every week in the pool, for free. I would give $20.00 worth of commissary food to the winner. That was really big to most of these inmates, since most of them had no money in their jail accounts. The funny thing about that is most every week a Hispanic guy would win the pool. Some of them don't even know anything about the sport, and that just goes to show how hard it is to pick the winners with the point spread in the NFL.

Soon, the dorm had a complete turnaround. The nightly fistfights were stopping. The Crips were interacting with the rest of the inmates, and a brotherhood—a sense of family—was starting to develop between the inmates. It got back to me that each ethnic group looked at me as the father and leader of the dorm. This had become so noticeable that all the correctional officers and administrators started to show me special respect and appreciation for what I had accomplished.

The last activity that I created really cracks me up. I called it bingo. I would take fifty small packs of sugar and number them from 1 to 50. I would then put them in this two-quart gallon plastic pail. I then would have all fifty inmates of the dorm come into the chow room. There, I would have a few of the leaders sit alongside me in the front of the room. I would have one guy shake the pail, and another would pick the sugar packet out of the pail with the number on it. A third guy would hold the prize I would give away for that drawing. I would give fifty prizes. The way each winning number would be decided is by the bunk number that you had. Now! Besides a prize being given each time a number came out, if your number was called three times, you would get *Bingo* and receive an additional $10.00 of commissary food. If your number came out four times, you would get *Super Bingo* and get $20.00 extra prize. It's funny; the only time a bed number came out four times, the inmate that was there left that afternoon.

We would play bingo every Tuesday night at 7:30 and all the inmates would look forward to it. It was so popular that everyone throughout the building started to talk about it. I found that really funny; so did most of the administrators. The funniest of all is when you would see two big, tough inmates say to each other, "Today is Tuesday. Tonight is bingo night!"

Yes, I have left my mark in the famous Rikers Island jail, I am sure. Nobody has ever run Bingo games before.

There is one correctional officer who's stuck out in my mind during my six months. She's the notorious Ms. Stevens. She has the reputation of being the roughest and toughest officer in our building. I guess that's why she was assigned to be our steady, every day officer, since our dormitory was considered the toughest in the building. In all the time that I have been here, nobody could get to first base with her. She is exceptionally strict with everyone. I would find it very funny when a new inmate would come into the dorm and ask a simple question, and she would go at them like a lion. For about my first three months, I made it a point to stay clear of her. I wasn't going to give her the opportunity to chop off my head.

Then one day she had to escort me to another part of the building. It was the first time I talked to her. Something came over me to kid with her, even though I saw that nobody was ever able to kid with her before. Well! From that day on, she showed me a special courtesy and respect that has touched me. The biggest courtesy that she's extended to me is to open the room that has the hot pot early. It means so much to me to be able to have a hot cup of coffee early in the morning. I think she gets a kick out of how grateful I am just to get a cup of hot water.

About a month ago, she found out I am writing a book. I gave her a couple of the chapters that I've written in here. To my surprise, she took the time to proofread and correct a lot of my spelling. I have no doubt that the courtesies that she has extended have come from her being touched from the spirit from *Beyond the Beyond*. And now, millions of people will read of the goodwill extended to me from the Lion of Rikers Island.

Nigger, Nigger, Nigger, Nigger, Nigger, Nigger, Nigger, Nigger, Nigger, Nigger.

That is all I hear from the young inmates. Every other word in their vocabulary is nigger. I asked a few young black guys why the inner city youth of today use such a terrible, offensive word. Their response is, "We really don't mean anything by it. To us, it's just a word." Every guy I asked told me that his parents would get mad when they heard him use that word. In every case, the young guys said that their parents told them how hard and long of a struggle it was to have our society denounce the word. Now, most people in America find that word offensive and derogatory. Whenever there are discussions on that subject on the TV, most times people won't even use that word. Instead, they refer to it as "the **N**-word."

I blame the rap music culture of today as one of the main reasons for the abusive use of that word. This is a word that would not be taken lightly in the *Beyond the Beyond*. I am confident that shortly after this book is published, the word "nigger" will no longer be overly abused.

ᑤᕝ *Chapter Nine* ᕟᑲ

S o, as I now write, I am a couple of days away from being released from Rikers Island Jail on bail. Family and friends have joined together to raise the million-dollar bail. My heart has been touched, seeing so many people coming to support me. As I knew destiny would have it, I am going to be able to continue my work on the story of *Beyond the Beyond* on the outside. Once I'm released, all of my time and energy must be put towards the writing of this book. I cannot worry about spending time on my defense for trial. All of that is destined to work out. So now, I'm going to go back to telling my story.

Reader, I hope I'm not confusing you with the way I'm writing my story. I told you I've never read a book, much less tried to write one. I did not ask for this task, but destiny has put in on my plate.

I believe I left off just coming home from prison. I talked John Mamone—who picked me up—into investing in the Doc Watch. So after Mamone dropped me off at my brother's house—I had lost my condo by having to go into prison—John insisted that I stay with him until I got on my feet.

I cannot believe the psychological and emotional adjustment that takes place when you get out of prison. I had heard of talk about this happening to inmates when they come home from doing some length of time in prison, but I couldn't imagine it happening to me. I was coming out as one of the strongest, most physically fit and mentally strong individuals around. But as I sat on my brother's living room sofa, I was emotionally and physically spent. I still can't believe how I felt. I had no control over my emotions for that first day, and I was physically exhausted from doing nothing. It took me a whole day to get back to normal.

The next few days I spent with family and friends. It was a start for bonding and establishing a new sense of closeness with my children. I came out of prison with a purpose: to make an effort to become close to my kids.

In the meantime, I was seeing old friends, including one called Chizzy. I told him about my invention of the Doc Watch. He told me that his younger brother, Frankie Vuono had just become the president of NFL Properties. That's the department of the National Football League that handles the licensing of products that are officially endorsed by the NFL. Well! My friend set up an appointment for my partner and me to see Frankie at his home. After Johnnie Mamone and I spoke to Frankie for about an hour about the Doc Watch, Frankie said, "Stop! Say no more. You are officially endorsed by the NFL." What he meant by that was that once we had the watch manufactured and ready for marketing and sales, then at that point he would have our product officially endorsed by the NFL. From that evening on, every time I spoke of the Doc Watch, I mentioned that we were endorsed from the NFL.

Now! After about a week, I called Johnny Serubo. Since he'd been released from the joint before me, we'd arranged that as soon as I came home and got settled, I would give him a call. This kid was in the inner circle of all the top businessmen in Philadelphia. I told him about the watch that I had invented while at the Danbury FCI. Johnny seemed really interested in the idea, and was excited to get involved. I told Johnny that my plans were to go to the Joe Weider Company, the biggest company for bodybuilding equipment and supplements. They also had a big publication—a bodybuilding magazine.

I knew that with their audience and marketing power in the fitness area, I was sure that if I could sell the company on the idea of the Doc Watch, we would have a tremendous financial success. So I decided to bring my ideas to the Weider Company, but I had no idea how to put myself in position to speak to the head honcho. I called one of the Weider Fitness Centers at random and asked for the main office number. It took numerous calls and finagling until I got to speak to the vice president of marketing. I talked him into meeting with me. The earliest he was able to fit me in his schedule was when he was going to be in Alabama, so I said fine, "I'll meet you in Alabama."

Just a day after making that appointment, I get a call from my ex-brother-in-law. He was a big executive for a large computer company. He was calling to ask me if I could try and collect money that a company owed. This was the second time he called with this kind of favor. The first time, I got lucky and found the guy who tried to steal a half-million dollars' worth of computer shit. I wound up sending it all back to my ex-brother-in-law's company.

Now, what were the odds that I had to go to Alabama for two reasons? Here I was, never having been to Alabama or the Deep South, and now I had to go to Alabama for two different reasons, both at the same time. Well! I took advantage of the opportunity, and made my ex-brother-in-law pay all the expenses for the Doc Watch appointment also. My partner, Mamone, was unable to make the trip, because he was tied up with his other business; so I had my friend, Eddie, come with me.

From the moment we arrived, everyone made fun of the way we talked with our New York accents. I was having fun breaking their balls by saying that Penn State had a better football team than the University of Alabama, and that Joe Paterno was a better coach than Bear Bryant. Wow! Was that getting them mad! Bear Bryant was a legend down there—the people lived for Alabama football.

The first stop was Huntsville to collect the money for my ex-brother-in-law's company. We checked into our hotel and made plans to go out to eat that evening. The next morning, we went to this guy's office to see about his outstanding debt. When we got there, we caught him by surprise. He didn't know what to say or how to react, so he told us to come back the next morning.

Now, for the few minutes that I had spoken to him, I had been a complete gentleman. I knew that it was completely illegal to threaten or try to strong-arm this guy. I had no intention of intimidating him. I was aware that would be illegal, and that I could get in trouble for those actions. My thought, though, was that when he saw two big men coming all the way from the New York area to collect the money, maybe we would get lucky and get the money he legitimately owed without resorting to threats.

So the next morning, when we went to his office, he was acting like he was in a good mood and like he was going to cut a check for the money owed. Then all of a sudden, he said to me, "What happens if I decide not to pay you? Are you going to break my legs?"

I answered, "You're the tough guy, not me. You're the thief, not me. You're the guy breaking the law trying to steal computers from my family. I'm the victim here, not you." Then I added, "We're just going to have to take legal actions in this matter."

I got up to leave, with my friend, Eddie, right behind me. As we walked outside this building and we were getting ready to get into our rental car, six detectives came up to us with guns drawn and pointed at our heads. When one of the detectives put his hand near my pocket, I pushed it away.

That's where I had about $9000.00 wrapped up with a rubber band. I always carried a large sum of money with me when I went on trips being that I didn't believe in credit cards.

It turned out that the guy who owed my ex-brother-in-law the money got cute and called the cops after our first visit. He told them that the New York mafia came to kill him. So the detectives handcuffed us and brought us down to the Huntsville Police Department. That's where some funny shit happened.

The first thing the detectives did was to check me out. Based on a few of the stories I've already told you, reader, I assume that they decided that I had ties to the mafia. That's all they had to hear. They started treating us like we were some kind of big members of the mafia. They were starting to call in some of the big shots of the city of Huntsville. I could see them peeking from the corner of a door. They were in awe thinking they were seeing some kind of big mobster in their city.

As ridiculous as it was, it was funny. They had nothing on us, because we had done nothing wrong; but they kept us there the entire day. It seemed like they enjoyed talking to us. I remember one detective saying to me, "When we first approached you with our guns pointed at your head and my hand went to your pocket, you pushed it away. We could have shot you, but you didn't care." He then asked, "When the cops arrest you in New York, do they try and steal the money that you're carrying?"

I then replied, "No, but from the stories I've heard of the Deep South, when a Yankee comes into town, that's what I thought you might do." He got a good laugh at that.

Now, as it was getting late into the afternoon, I told them they had to let us go because I had an appointment that evening and it was a couple of hours away by car. When I told them what the appointment was all about the Doc Watch, my new invention, and that I was meeting with the vice president of the Joe Weider Company, they were interested. But it wasn't until I started to bullshit them and tell them that I was scheduled to go on the Johnny Carson show in two weeks to talk about it that they got excited. I told them that I'd mention the detectives of the city of Huntsville, how they were so professional and courteous, and the hospitality they extended to me. I told them that I was impressed with law enforcement in my first experience in the Deep South. After those compliments, they decided to let us go.

We rushed back to our hotel to shower and get dressed for the Doc Watch appointment. This is where I it gets really funny. As I was in the shower, there was a knock on the door. When I answered the door, soaking wet, with just a towel around me, five detectives came marching into the room. Each one handed me a business card with his name on it. After the last detective gave me his card, the boss said to me, "If you're ever back in Huntsville, stop in and see us. We'll put out the red carpet for you." Well! It was wasn't until we were driving to the Doc Watch appointment that I realized that they came to the hotel to give us their personal cards so I would mention their names, individually, on the Johnny Carson show. Oh, well! I think if I ever go back to Huntsville, Alabama, they'll tar and feather me.

Now we were in the rental car on a two-hour ride to meet the Vice President of Marketing for the Joe Weider Company. To my surprise, when we got there, besides the Vice President, was Eric Weider, the son of Ben Weider, the president of the Company. The meeting went really well!

When I was through with my presentation, they said they were very interested in my idea, but had an even greater interest in trying to get me to consider an executive position in their sales department. Eric Weider said to me, "I'm impressed with your bodybuilding watch idea, but I'm even more impressed with your dynamic sales ability."

They set up an appointment for me to go out to California to speak in front of the Board of Directors. All the directors from all over the country were meeting in three months, so I had to anxiously wait for the meeting.

In the meantime, I planned a trip to visit my mom and dad in Boynton Beach, Florida. During my incarceration, they had sold their home in New Jersey and retired to Florida. This was the first time I ever went to Florida and the first time I saw my mom and dad in the four years since my incarceration. I arrived there on a Saturday, and when Sunday dinner came around, I was surprised to see all my aunts and uncles coming over to eat. When my mom had moved to this retirement development, all the aunts and uncles on my mother's side decided to follow her and get condos in the same development. She was the rock of the family—the one who had always kept the family close.

So, family Sundays still hadn't changed. The food that was on that table could have fed an army. All the varieties of Italian specialty dishes would be there, just the same as I remembered from back when I was a little boy. Everyone in the family and all our friends knew that Sunday was my mother's day. Church and an all-day feast was the Sunday routine for as long as I could remember, and everybody was always invited.

During that one week trip, I overheard a conversation between my mom and dad and learned that my mom was having some back pain. They assured me it was nothing to be concerned about. So, I went back to Jersey and started doing some construction work with the carpenters' union waiting for the Doc Watch appointment.

It seemed like those three months flew by quick, and soon, John Mamone and I were on the plane, flying to Woodland Hills, California, home of headquarters for Joe

Weider Company. We arrived a day early so we went to visit the Universal Studios. I remember going on this tiny train, taking a tour of the studio. There were two things I saw that especially got my attention. One was when we went through this body of water, which we were told was where they filmed the parting of the red sea in the movie, *The Ten Commandments*. The second thing that got my special attention was when I saw the mechanical shark that they used for the movie *Jaws*. I really enjoyed that day even more, because I never took the time to go anywhere. In the past, all my time had been spent on gambling on sports, TV, or in the casinos.

The next morning we arrived a little early at the Weider headquarters. As we are waiting in their beautiful lobby to be called to address the board of directors, I noticed this large American flag in a huge glass case on the wall. The little metal plate at the bottom of the frame said that this was one of the first American flags ever made. I was in awe. I carefully looked at the workmanship of the thirteen stars and the red and blue stripes. I couldn't help but think about how this flag, when it had been made, represented a brand-new country that had become the greatest nation on Earth. I was so mesmerized by that flag that when the receptionist called us to go into the meeting room for our presentation, I had to quickly refocus my mind to the Doc Watch.

My partner and I walked into an elaborate meeting hall where about thirty people were seated. Eric Weider introduced me to speak on the Doc Watch. Ironically, I believe it was my worst presentation of the Doc Watch, but definitely good enough to sell them on my idea. The sight of that flag had totally made me lose my focus on my preparation for my presentation.

After I had spoken, John Mamone and I went into the coffee room where we waited for Eric Weider. About fifteen minutes later, he walked into the room, smiling and saying, "We like your idea. Give us a week, and we'll get in touch with you."

So, Mamone and I flew back to New Jersey, optimistic that the trip was a success. Sure enough, about a week later, Eric Weider gave me a call. He said, "We want to get involved and be part of your bodybuilding watch, but we want to go slow. The first step is for you to get a prototype watch and then research the cost to have it manufactured."

I replied, "Okay, I'll work on it." I was somewhat disappointed, because I wanted them to get more involved, so they would have done everything.

The next week, just as we just started research how to get a prototype watch made up, I got a call from Johnny Serubo. He was all excited, saying to me, "I hope you didn't make a deal with the Weider Company. I have a close friend that I do business with. He's the president of one of the largest TV infomercial companies in the country, and he's really interested in your idea. He wants to meet with you.

He's located in Philadelphia. If he gets involved with the watch, they'll do everything. They'll manufacture, market, and distribute the watch. You will have to do nothing but get a check every month."

Wow! That's what I was really looking for. So I told Serubo to make the appointment, and I decided to blow off the Weider Company for the time being.

So, a couple of weeks later, Mamone and I were in Philadelphia giving our presentation of the Doc Watch. I believe the name of the infomercial company was Metromedia, but I'm not sure. Anyway, the president of the company and, naturally, Serubo were there, along with members of the board. I remember seeing a few inventors of some really popular, successful items there.

My presentation went really well. I was at my best. I was on a roll! I remember the president of the company trying to ask me a question, and I wouldn't let him speak. Everyone in the room, including him, got a kick out of that.

When I had finished my presentation, Mamone and I went to wait in their coffee room. Shortly after, Serubo walked into the room shaking his head and saying, "Wow! The president wants to invite you for dinner. He's never invited any presenter for dinner before." I was happy to hear that and, naturally, accepted.

So we went to a fine Philly restaurant. As we were at the bar having a drink while we were waiting to be seated, the president—I forget his name—was telling us a story. As he got into his story, I interrupted him to ask him a question. He replied like a little boy, "Wait a minute! You wouldn't let me talk when you were speaking, so now you can't interrupt me. You're on my time."

It was so funny the way he had said it that I gave him a big hug and said, "You're right! I can't interrupt you."

The evening went well, and he said, "While your idea of your product doesn't fit 100% into our formula, we really like your idea, and we're going to seriously consider it."

It was about two weeks before Serubo got back to me on what had been decided. He told me, "The president and the board went back and forth with the idea for these past two weeks even though it doesn't fit into their formula. After everything was finally said and done, they decided to pass on the idea. Their final decision was based on the fact that their formula was working 100% with all their other products, so they didn't want to go against their formula. I was extremely disappointed with the news, but my positive attitude overcame the disappointment.

⌒ *Chapter Ten* ⌒

Shortly after that disappointing news, I got a call from my dad to tell me that the doctors discovered that my mother had bone cancer. When I heard that, I immediately jumped on a plane and went to Florida. The last thing on my mind was to go back to working on the Doc Watch for the Weider Company.

When I got down there, my mother was in good spirits and especially happy to see me. On this trip, I spent every minute with my mom and dad. The memories of the love shared between my mom and dad has been locked in my heart and soul. I remember how hard my mother would try to hide the pain she was enduring in front of me, even though I had been told that bone cancer is the most painful. She was more concerned with me than herself.

After spending two months down there, I really had to get back home to take care of a couple of things. As I was saying my goodbyes, my mother hugged me, told me she loved me and said, "Paulie, I will never leave you."

Reader, remember these words!

After about three weeks back in Jersey, I get a phone call from my father. He said, "Paulie, I think you should come down here. I had to put your mother in Hospice." That was all he had to say. I was on the next flight to Florida. When I arrived, my uncle came to the airport to pick me up. We immediately went to Hospice where my brothers and Dad were waiting by my mother's bedside. My mother was heavily sedated and sleeping.

My father looked totally exhausted. So many months of tireless and endless care that my dad had given my mom had taken their toll. Even since the day my mom was put in Hospice, my dad was there twenty-four hours a day. He was sleeping on the lounge chair that was in my mom's room.

I was so happy that I could give my father a break and let him go back home to get a good night's sleep. I ended up staying there twenty-four hours a day for the next two weeks. During that whole time, my mom was heavily sedated to control the pain. But one day, in a half-conscious state, she started talking to me about the *Blessed Virgin Mary* and *Jesus Christ*. She was saying, "I should love them with all my heart."

Reader, again, I ask you to remember this for later as we go on!

Now, after two weeks of this routine, my nephew, Joe—a high school football coach—said to me, "Hey, Unc. I have a surprise for you. How would you like to go and see your favorite football team, Penn State, and your favorite football coach, Joe Paterno? They're playing the Miami Hurricanes in the Orange Bowl. The teams are ranked number one and number two in the country. Before the game, we'll have breakfast with the Miami Hurricanes football team, and then we'll watch the game on the Miami Hurricanes sidelines."

Well, I couldn't believe what I was hearing! Along with boxing, college football was my favorite sport to watch. For thirty years, I'd been a big-time fan of college football, and I'd never gone to a single game. Now, I had the opportunity to see the biggest game of the season, and my favorite team and coach—not to mention, on the sidelines.

Even though it was too good to be true, I said, "As good as it sounds, Joe, I don't want to leave Grandma."

When my father and brothers heard that, they got mad and said, "You need a break! We want you to go."

So I said, "Okay, Joe. I'll go."

Then my nephew said, "There's just one catch, Unc."

And then I said, "I knew it! I knew it was too good to be true."

Joe told me, "It's no big deal. All you have to do is wear my high school football hat and shirt, and pretend you're a coach."

When I heard that, I said, "Okay Joe. I can handle that."

So, when Saturday came, off we went to the game!

We were in the cafeteria, getting ready to have breakfast with the Miami Hurricanes football team. This is when something funny happened to me. As I was in line with my tray to get breakfast, I got this big slap on the back. When I turned to see who slapped me, it turned out to be one of the Miami assistant football coaches. He said to me, "So, coach. How did your team make out last night?"

I didn't know what to say! In that split second, I tried to think of a hundred different answers to get out of it, but couldn't find one. So I slapped him back and said, "I'm no fucking coach. My nephew is the coach. I just came down with him."

He laughed and said, "That's okay. Just enjoy the game."

After breakfast, we went down on the field. Penn State was starting to warm up. Within a minute, who do I see, but Joe Paterno? Wow! Did that excite me! He was one of only a few heroes that I have. I followed him around the field, staying about ten feet from him, until I finally got the courage to go up to him. I said, "Coach, I love you. I love everything you stand for. You're my idol! Penn State is my favorite team, but I'm stuck on the Miami sidelines—but I'll be quietly rooting for you."

He laughed and said, "Thanks for the compliments."

I wanted to tell him that I'd been betting on Penn State for thirty years, despite them never covering the point spread but I didn't have the balls. I thought he might get mad if I mentioned gambling.

The game turned out great! The score went back and forth until, with a couple of minutes left, the Hurricanes scored to win the game. They ended up winning the National Championship that year.

That was the first and only time I went to a college football game. Wow! It was some experience. I had forgotten about all the sorrow that I was going through for that one day.

⟬ *Chapter Eleven* ⟭

So the next day, I went back to Hospice to be with my mom. This was going to be her last, final week; and during this week, the greatest love story that I could have possibly imagined seeing would unfold. The last week, she was in and out of it, but the way she responded to my father was incredible.

It was Saturday night, and she was slowly leaving us. We were actually praying for God to take her. Isn't life crazy? Here's someone you love more than life itself, and you're praying for that person to pass on.

At about 11:00 Saturday night, my dad, my brother, John, and I left my mother's room to go into the lounge. They had these comfortable couches where we could rest. We were so exhausted that we were ready to pass out. We all wound up falling asleep for almost an hour.

All of a sudden, out of a sound sleep, my father jumped up off the couch and started walking real fast down the hall and into my mom's room. That woke my brother, John and I, so we started to quickly follow my father. When we got into the room, my mother was silent. My father took her hand and put it in between his two hands and started to rub it. His bald head and face became redder than a red light bulb. She started to breathe heavily as he continued to rub her hand, and within seconds, she took her last breath.

At that very moment that I saw her take her last breath, I saw a flash of light leave her body. This was the second time I saw that flash of a light leave like that. Even though it was the second time, I was sure it was my imagination. A minute later, we called the nurse to check her heart and the nurse confirmed that she had passed on. The official time that they had put for her passing on was, 12:01 a.m., making it Sunday morning: her day.

To my brother and me, it was obvious that my mother's spirit had awakened my father out of a sound sleep within a minute of her spirit leaving us. She wanted us to be there with her before she left to go on her journey to the *Beyond the Beyond*. This isn't just something I believe: *It's something that I know!*

I spent about two weeks with my dad and brothers after my mom's passing. Then I left Florida to go back to Jersey. Shortly after being back home, I heard that two old friends of mine that I played high school football with, John Daly and Bobby Liscio, had become the shift manager and the casino manager of the Sands Hotel and Casino in Atlantic City. So, for the next fifteen years, I started going exclusively to that casino. The Sands eventually became my second home. I lived there almost as much as I did at my home.

One time I planned a six-day trip to Atlantic City to stay at the Sands Casino. I had invited my two brothers, John and Mark, to come with me. John had to fly in from Florida where he lives. I paid for my brother John's airplane ticket, and everything else was going to be compliments of either myself or the Sands Casino. That would include beautiful penthouse suites, gourmet restaurants, and shows and entertainment.

My nephews and one of my sons, Brian, came down to spend a couple of days with us. Mark and I picked John up at the Atlantic City Airport. It was really convenient; it was just a ten-minute ride from the casino to the airport. This was the first time in many, many years that all three of us brothers were together at the same time. I told my brothers that our mother's spirit was happy that we were all together.

Each day, I told my brothers how strongly I felt our mother's presence, and that her spirit was happy that I had brought the family together. In the meantime, each day I was losing between $1,000 and $2,000 gambling; but every day, I told my brothers that our mother's spirit wasn't going to let me lose any money for the trip. I told them her spirit wasn't going to make me win, but she really wouldn't let me lose. I told them that every time I have a feeling about our mother's spirit, it happens.

The days went by, and we were having a great time, especially when all our kids came down to meet us. The laughs we had were priceless. The joy of my mother's spirit seeing her grandsons and sons all together was incredibly strong. But every day, I just keep losing, right to the final day. The day we were getting ready to leave to take John to the airport, between tips and gambling for the week, I was down $9,600.

As we were driving to the airport, I said what I had said every day for the entire trip: that I couldn't believe that my mother's spirit would make me lose money on this trip. I told them I couldn't believe it, but I was wrong.

My kid brother and I dropped our older brother at the airport. As we were driving to the parkway to start our two-hour drive to get back home, Mark asked me, "Do you have to do anything when you get home?" When I told him no, he said, "Me neither. Do you want to stay the rest of the day at the Sands? We can leave early tomorrow morning to go back home."

I answered, "Okay. It's crazy to leave now. It'll be late by the time we get home, and we have nothing to do. You're right. We'll leave early tomorrow morning."

Neither one of us gave any further thought to our mother's spirit and what I had said for the last six days. In my mind, it was a foregone conclusion that my feelings had been wrong, and that was the end of it.

So Mark and I went back to the Sands. We hung out in the room for about an hour before I decided to go down to the Casino to play. Mark said, "Wait for me, and I'll come down and watch you play," so we both went down.

I played at the blackjack table for about an hour with Mark sitting by my side, watching me play. All of a sudden, out of nowhere, I heard my mother's spirit telling me to go to the roulette table and to get the money I'd lost.

At that very second, I jumped, and my brother got scared when he saw my face. I told him, "Mother's spirit spoke to me. She told me to play her birthday."

(Reader, I am crying as I am writing this, and the chills are going right through me. I cannot help it. This happens every time I tell this story.)

We walked over to the roulette table. On the first spin, I put $70 on number 6, my mother's birthday. It came out on the very first spin, just as my mother's spirit told me it would. I won $2,400.

Now I was sure that I wasn't nuts or fuckin delusional. I knew my mother's spirit had called me at that very moment. So I started yelling at the top of my voice, "Everyone come over here, and watch my mother's spirit. I guarantee you that number 6 will come out again and repeat. It's destiny."

A big crowd started to form because of how I was screaming. When all the big casino bosses came over and saw it was me, they were shocked. I had been the most liked, respected, and low-key player in the Sands for twenty years. As that crowd was watching, I put the maximum bet of $200 straight up on number 6. I started yelling in a deep, stern voice, "Everyone, come watch number 6 come out! Come and watch destiny. I guarantee it."

I then turned to the croupier (that's the person who spins the ball) and said, "I want you to go out of your way to try and spin the ball so it'll go into a different section. I want you to try your hardest to try and make the ball not even get close to the section of number 6." I then said at the top of my lungs, "No matter how you spin the ball, it's guaranteed to go into number 6! It's destiny—my mother's spirit told me." I then told the dealer to spin the ball.

The crowd anxiously waited. The ball was going around and around. As it was ready to land, it was on the side of the wheel opposite from where the number 6 was, when all of a sudden, the ball hit a prong—that's the little divider between the numbers—and ricocheted all the way to the other side of the wheel and into number 6. Everyone couldn't believe their eyes! Most people were sick that they hadn't played number 6.

Mark and I started to cry as we were punching each other out of the emotion we were feeling. We fell down and we were rolling around the floor, crying and hugging each other. The big casino bosses came over and asked, "Doc, are you all right?"

I replied, "Yes! It has nothing to do with the money I won. I'm all emotional over something that is much, much more important than the money."

Reader, I'm not through with the story!

On the first hit on number 6, I won $2,400. On the second hit on number 6, I won $7,200. You add it up and it comes to $9,600. That's the exact amount that it had cost me for the trip!

If you remember, I told my brothers that our mother's spirit wasn't going to make me win, but she wasn't going to let me lose, either. When we called our brother, John, in Florida, and told him the story, he started to cry. He said he truly believed in the power of my mother's spirit.

This is when I was starting to become aware of my connection to the *Beyond the Beyond*.

☙ *Chapter Twelve* ❧

A round the time that I first started going to the Sands, I had a lawyer friend of mine, Al Porro, doing some legal work for me on the Doc Watch. He was also working on putting together a deal to open this big nightclub very close to Giants Stadium. He also owned a go-go joint next to Giants Stadium. In fact, that was the place I mentioned earlier—the place where I had taken over the food end of that business.

Anyway, Al was trying to get Lawrence "LT" Taylor, the great football player for the New York Giants, to get involved. Lawrence was one of the most popular players in all of sports at that time. Lawrence frequently went into the go-go joint to have a good time with the girls.

So, I found out that Taylor's best friend, Paul Davis, was looking to buy Al's go-go joint. I believe he was looking to do that so LT would have his own playground with the go-go girls. So I tipped Al off that if he made a deal on the go-go joint, LT would get involved in the nightclub, and allow the club to be named LT's. I knew this because LT and Paul Davis hinted to me they would be interested in taking over the go-go joint.

I remember the grand opening of LT's Sports Lounge. You could've barely fit in the place because of all the sports celebrities who showed up that night. I have one memory that night of when LT, a number of his personal friends, and I were in the office having a drink, trying to get a break from the incredible crowd. A guy came up to me and made a somewhat sarcastic remark about my tuxedo. (By the way, the grand opening was a black-tie affair.) I was wearing a gray tuxedo, and everyone else was wearing a black tux. I believe the remark was, "Is your tuxedo polyester?" I bit my tongue and decided not to say anything. My intention was to grab him at the end of the night.

I finished my drink and left the office. Within seconds of me leaving the office, this guy comes running up to me, nervously saying, "I'm so sorry for what I said. Please accept my apology. Lawrence just told me you're the last person here that I should be insulting. Please, please accept my apology."

I replied to him, "You did the right thing," and then shook his hand. It turned out that this guy was LT's golf buddy from whenever he spent time in Florida. LT's sports bar was the hottest place in the area for the first year before it started to fizzle out.

About six months later, LT did a favor for me. One of my friends asked me if I would ask Lawrence if he would do a favor and sign some autographs for a grand opening at a furniture store in New York State. I was told it would be just for a couple of hours, and that there would be only a couple of hundred people there. Lawrence said he would.

The grand opening was on a Saturday, and we got there late. Well! When we arrived there, there were thousands upon thousands of people who showed up. When Lawrence first saw that, he got scared. He said, "There's no security here."

I told him, "Don't worry. My friends and I will be your security."

He wound up signing autographs for the entire day, until his arm was ready to fall off. A short time later, I heard rumors that because of that favor, people were making inferences that LT was tied to the mob.

ᴄᴡᴏ *Chapter Thirteen* ᴄᴡᴏ

Here I go again! I have to stop writing about my life story, because I have to speak of current events. I have just awakened out of a sound sleep. It's 3:00 in the morning. I spent yesterday morning and all day at a close friend's funeral. His name is Richie Pezzolla—you may remember him as Richie P, from earlier in the book.

I can't spend too much time writing about him, although he deserves it, because there's still too much of my story left to tell. For the last year, Richie suffered from liver cancer. A good part of that time is when I was incarcerated. As you have already read, it took numerous miracles for me to have gotten out on bail, but I know that destiny brought me home for his last final days. Richie P. was a truly loved guy in our hometown and the immediate area. I don't think there's a person who can say a bad thing about him. He was active in all the sports programs in our town and kept six decades of our hometown athletes close together.

For the two days of his wake, the lines of people who'd come to pay their respects stretched far outside the door of the funeral home. But everyone waited in the freezing cold of these January winter days. People could only wish that they could be eulogized the way he was.

Yesterday, the day of the funeral, the precession was so long with cars that many couldn't even get close to the cemetery. Now, Richie P.'s body has been put in the frozen earth, and soon he will be forgotten. It might take a couple of decades for family and close friends to slowly lose his memory, but like every other person, that is what will happen. Yes, there are a few people whose memory lives on, like Michelangelo or George Washington. It could be for one hundred years or a thousand years, but it's all a drop in a bucket when we speak of *eternity*. And when we get down to it, what is a memory, if that's all there is to eternity?

Reader, I'm sure you know that we will get back to this.

Back to my story. So now I was going exclusively to the Sands Casino, since my friends were running the joint. After my blackjack card-counting days, I could never get back to card-counting. It was too much work and stress, and mentally I couldn't handle it. So now, for years, I just played blackjack using basic strategy. Basic strategy is a system that lets you bring the odds to almost even with the house. Now my strategy was to play within my means. What I mean by that is that my wagering bets would be just a very small part of the money I had in my pocket.

Blackjack is a game of sequences. When you're playing basic strategy, you're on a seesaw that goes up and down. I would usually quit each week while I was up. In the meantime, I was living in the casino for free, having gourmet dinners, and seeing fine entertainment, all compliments of the casino. The casinos evaluate a player based on the time that player puts into gambling. The action you give the casino will determine what complimentary services you are entitled to. "The action" refers to the amount of money you are risking, and the amount of time that you are putting into playing. Between the two, your playing time is more important to the casino than the amount you bet. If a player is wagering large sums of money, but just for a short time, they could get lucky and hurt the casino. But when a player is putting in some substantial time, it's benefiting the house because of the mathematical odds the casino has.

Putting in the time was never a problem for me. By playing perfect basic strategy, I would go back and forth with the casino and rarely lose, but at the same time, I would be giving them all the action they wanted.

Here is a funny story. On one particular trip, I had stayed at the Sands for over a week's time. When I went back the following week, one of the pit bosses came up to me and started laughing. He said, "You broke the record. You put more playing time in playing blackjack in a seven-day period than anyone at the Sands. When you finally left last week, I went into the computer and added up all the hours that you had played. You beat the old record held by a professor from Penn State by an hour."

Well, I really made him laugh when I said, "One of those playing sessions had lasted two and a half days! What finally made me go up to my room to sleep was when I was dealt a twenty—a jack and a queen—and I saw them dancing on the green felt blackjack table. They were doing the waltz, cheek-to-cheek. They looked so in love as they were dancing across the table. That's when I decided to quit playing and go to sleep. I was hallucinating."

Many people have laughed at that story.

During this time, my girlfriend, Angie, and I split up. I moved in with my close friend, Louis Morella. Louie and I had gotten close the last couple of years, and I was taking him on most of my trips to Atlantic City. Louis was about six years younger than I am. He grew up in my hometown. Some people might say he was a little slow, and maybe that's so; but in certain ways, he was really smart. Everyone in our hometown liked him because he was so pure of heart.

It was only about a year after his mom and dad passed away that I started to get very close with him. In a short time, he became like my baby brother, or maybe like my son. I truly loved him. After really never going anywhere up to his late thirties, he spent the next seven years living in casinos with me. I was taking care of him. I told everyone he was my driver, but the truth is that I drove because he was a really bad driver. Sure, I had a reputation of being a bad driver—all my friends would make fun of me and say I couldn't see—but I thought he was worse than me.

Louie was tall, dark, and handsome. He walked around the Sands casino like he owned it, and everyone treated him with the utmost respect, because of me. For seven years, I had Louie living like a king: penthouses, fine dining, and shows. I would even get him hookers whenever he wanted.

I went to West Point for the graduation of my son, Marcus. I got to see the president of the United States, President Clinton, hand my son his college diploma. As I was watching the President shaking his hand, I asked myself, *"Why am I so lucky? Why am I so blessed to have four healthy children, and all of them on the right path?"* Even though my ex-wife, Louise, deserves all the credit, they are my children.

My dad was at the graduation, too. As the president called Marcus' name, my father started to cry, saying, "If only your mother could have lived to see this." Little did he know that *she was there*. I heard her voice and she spoke to me throughout the ceremony. Naturally, I could never say this to anyone.

At the moment, I'm stuck on what I should write about next. I have to get through my life story so that I can get to the real purpose of the writing of this book. Up until this point, my writing has just flowed. I know that I'm spiritually motivated in my writings, because no matter what I choose to write about at the time, there's some incredible relevance for telling that story at just that time.

I'll give you just a couple of examples. I wrote about seeing the movie about Stanley Tookie-Williams, the co-founder of the notorious Crips. Shortly after that, I was incarcerated and living in real life amongst the Crips. I left off just now starting to tell you about my beloved friend, Louis Morella, and today turned out to be the day of his anniversary of his passing. I wasn't aware of that until it dawned on me after I started to write about him. I will get back to Louie's passing on as I go forward.

There have been two people that I've felt spiritually connected to since I started writing this book. They are Don Imus and Oprah Winfrey. How ironic that they are two of the most powerful people, when it comes to the marketing of a book. I will get back to them later in my story.

I have this feeling that I want to breeze through the rest of my life story so that I can get to the purpose of the writing of this book. I know my feelings are spiritually motivated, so I have to go with my feelings. I have to completely finish my personal story so you, reader, will know who the person is that's telling the story of *Beyond the Beyond*.

I'm trying to do this mission with common sense. I've always called myself the doctor of common sense. There's a quote that I heard that I just love and believe is true: "Common sense is not very common."

Anyway, let me get back to my story. I'll try and get it out of the way as quickly as I can. So around this time in my story is when I'm really being labeled a member of the mafia. My picture is in color on the front page of the largest newspaper in New Jersey—the *Star-Ledger*. I'm in the photo talking to my co-defendant, John Mamone, in the courtroom. By the way, that picture was also in all the New Jersey newspapers. If you read the newspapers, you couldn't miss it.

There had been a large number of guys that were arrested along with John Mamone and me. The charges were a broad list of allegations. The main charge of the indictment was against a guy named George Weingarten. He was being charged with the murder of John DiGilio. DiGilio was alleged to be a boss of the Genovese crime family in North Jersey. My charge turned out to be some really ridiculous thing. The charge was really bogus, so let me briefly tell you the story.

Around that time, I decided I want to get back to trying to get the Doc Watch off the ground. So Mamone and I were back in contact with each other, trying to see where we could get a prototype of the watch made up. One day when we were together working on the watch, John asked me to take a ride with him. Mamone was in trucking and construction. So we go to this guy's construction office—I don't know the guy's name. John asked me to come in rather than wait in the car, so I went in. As John went in his office, I waited in the lobby. After a few minutes, I heard this loud scuffle, so I went running into the office to break it up at the same time that his secretary came running in from another office. She was hysterical, and she was screaming! I told her to calm down.

To this day, I don't know what the argument was about. I didn't care then, and I don't care now. After I broke the scuffle up, they calmly talked for about a minute, and then we left. Well! Immediately after we left, the secretary called the police. The way it turned out, the construction deal that they were discussing was part of the indictment. The bottom line is that the reason I was indicted was because the secretary said I threatened her. I believe she said I would "break her legs." Not only is that totally false, but it really pissed me off.

Remember, I told you earlier, reader, that one of my strongest beliefs is to never disrespect a woman, much less threaten a woman with bodily harm. My belief is that if you want to be a tough guy, go be a tough guy with another man, not a woman.

Well! The way all this bullshit ended was when the main defendant, George Weingartner, committed suicide. The prosecutor no longer had any real interest in the case, so they offered all the rest of the defendants deals. When my court-appointed attorney came to me and said I could have a deal for three years' probation, stupid me, I said, "Okay, I'll take it. What do I care about being on probation? I don't do anything wrong."

Only after I was in front of the judge to take my plea was I sorry. When I heard him saying that I was copping out to some kind of threat to a woman, I got really angry and wanted to take back that plea, because it was not true. But I said to myself, "Fuck it. Let me just get this over with and keep my mouth shut." So now, because of the bullshit story, all the newspapers have me publicized as a mobster.

After all that bullshit happened, whenever I went to the Sands, everyone thought I was some kind of big mafia man. It would have really bothered me, but everyone still treated me with the same respect that they had always showed me. I have always demanded respect for my whole life, but I believe very strongly that to have the right to demand respect, you have to give respect. I guess that's why one of my favorite quotes from the Bible is something Jesus

Christ said: *Do unto others as you would want them to do unto you.*

I remember a time when I was playing roulette. I just kept playing this one number—I forget what the number was. Well, anyway, there was this guy standing next to me, and on each spin, he kept rooting for me to hit the number. After a short time, the number came out. I remember winning $2,000. Well, when I hit, he came over acting excited, and gave me a hug.

It turned out that he pickpocketed me for $8,600 that I had in my front pocket. In the few minutes that it took for me to notice, he was long gone. When top management of the Sands heard about what happened, they came to me and said, "Because of the respect we have for you, and your high credibility, we are going to give you a special $2,500 refund check. This is something we normally never do—it's the highest amount that we have the power to do—and this can only be done in very special circumstances, but we want to do it for you."

Around this time, I got a call from a cousin of mine, Joey, who lived in Florida. He told me that he had a friend from down there who would like to make an appointment to meet with me. So a week later, this guy flew up to Jersey and we met. The guy's name was Donnie Platten. It turned out that he was originally from Jersey, and had grown up the next town over from me. When we met after talking for a short time, it turned out that our mothers knew each other and had been friends.

He wanted to meet me because he was aware that I had owned health spas and he was looking for my expertise in that area. At that moment, he was looking to put together a group of investors to start a health spa chain in the state of Florida—actually on the eastern part of the state, in the Boca Raton area where he lived. The way it turned out, within a very short time after our meeting, the potential investors' deal fell through.

Nevertheless, we started to get close. This guy was an interesting character. When he went back to Florida, he would call me every day, seven days a week, talking to me for at least an hour every day. The conversations were all about his new ideas for opening different businesses. Every day he would call me, all excited about his new business ideas. After a little while, I started to think he was fucking nuts, but he was a creative person, intelligent, a really good public speaker, and a pretty good salesman.

Well! After a couple of months, as it happened, Donnie arranged for me to meet his sister, Marie. The purpose for our meeting, from what I remember, had to do with a clothing business deal he was trying to put together with his sister. He wanted me to get involved. By the way, she lived in Jersey, in the next town over from me, actually in the same house where they'd grown up.

So I took her out for dinner, and that started a relationship that has lasted for the last fifteen years, up to the present day of my writing. Most people who know us cannot believe that two people who are so opposite in one breath, and then so much alike in the next, could ever last in a loving relationship. I guess the mysteries of love are hidden deep inside the heart.

Marie is small in stature but has a heart as big as an elephant. Despite her cute, petite, adorable little figure, she has the temper of a furious lion. After everything is said and done, despite her tiny little hands and feet, nobody could find anyone with a bigger heart or a more loyal friend than Marie.

I believe most couples have some kind of special nickname for each other. I started referring to her as Boosch. Don't ask me how I come up with that name. One day, it was just the way I felt—it came to me to call her Boosch, and I have been referring to her by that name ever since.

Now Boosch and I had been going out for about six months when we started going on trips to Florida. We would go see her brother and my father. From the very first time my dad met Boosch, he had a special liking for her. She used to really make him laugh. Within a short time, they established a very special connection with each other, and that made me very happy.

We often went to Florida, both to hear about Donnie's business ideas, and also to spend time with my father. Now during this period, my special friend, Louie Morella, moved out and went to move in with his girlfriend. The first month that he moved out we didn't see each other, but just spoke to each other on the phone.

Well! When he stopped over to visit, I couldn't believe the weight he'd lost. He told me he was on a diet. As the weeks went by and I saw he was still losing weight, I got concerned and said, "I'm going to take you to the doctor. I want you to get a checkup."

When the doctor, who was a friend of mine, got through examining him, he said to me, "I want you to take him to this specialist. I don't like what I see."

At this point, I didn't say anything to Louis about the concern. So we went to see the specialist. After a short time examining and testing Lou, the doctor blew me out of the water by saying, "Louis has six months to live. He has cancer throughout his body."

I can so clearly remember the sorrow and the tears Marie and I both shed, to see this child-like, beautiful person in a man's body facing life's ultimate destiny. When the doctor came and told me that he was going to tell Louie, I replied, "I think that's not a good idea. Knowing Louis the way that I know him, I believe that to tell him that news straight-out wouldn't be right."

I remember the doctor getting mad at me and saying, "I have to tell him. I have to go in the office and talk to him." I was nervous, not knowing what was going to happen. I anxiously waited for the door to open. When Louis came out of the office, he sat with Marie, and the doctor called me into his office. He said, "After talking to Louis for a few minutes, I see that you're right. I'm going to let you handle it your way."

I was so grateful to hear the doctor say that. Only I knew how pure of heart Louis was, and that God would give me the wisdom and compassion to deal with him as he went toward his final destination. I remember during those last couple of months, Louie would ask me, "Am I going to get better, or am I going to be put in a box?"

I would reply to him, "We're all in God's hands. We all have the same ultimate destiny. Your health is in God's hands." This is how I chose to deal with the situation. I have such strong belief that God had given me the wisdom to handle it right, because I've never seen a stronger and braver person facing his final days.

In Louie's last final hours, Boosch and I were by his bedside, praying and talking to him. I remember Marie saying, "You're going to be with your mom and dad in Heaven, Lou."

I told him, "You're the bravest and toughest man I've ever met"

Then he started to breathe really heavy before he passed on. At that moment, again, I saw this flash of light leave his body. I was too embarrassed to tell Marie because I didn't want her to think I'm nuts. But this was the third time I was in the presence of someone taking their last breath—my uncle Lou, my mom, and then Louie—and saw this flash of a light at the moment of death. Even though it was now three times, I was convinced that it was my imagination. My common sense said I shouldn't tell this to anyone, not even my closest loved ones.

We buried Louis on his birthday, six months after that first doctor's visit. The emotional pain that I was enduring from the loss of Louis shortly turned into physical pain from a car accident. It was a rainy morning. I was at the bottom of a ramp with my car completely stopped, getting ready to go onto the highway, when a concrete truck came sliding down the ramp and crashed into the back of my car. The power of the impact totaled my car and snapped my neck back. I damaged one of my top vertebrae.

For the next year, the pain I endured was unbearable. At the time, I didn't have any kind of medical coverage, so as each month went by, I just kept hoping that my injury would go away and that the pain would subside. Unfortunately, that didn't happen. The pain just continued to escalate. It got to a point where I was in so much pain that I felt I didn't want to live anymore.

I always thought I had a low tolerance to pain—that when it came to pain, I was a big baby—but from time to time, I would question if that was true. "I asked myself, *how do we measure pain? How do we measure pain from one person to the next? How do we really measure one person's pain tolerance compared to the next person's pain tolerance?*" Maybe today's science has the answer, but it is always something I asked myself. It's funny to me that whenever I'm on the subject of one's health, there is a quote that I remember that always comes to mind: "Good health is a king's crown on a well man's head that only a sick person can see."

Well! I could relate to that. I always took my good health for granted. It was only when I had a toothache or a sprained ankle that I realized how happy I was just not to be in pain.

Finally, a friend recommended me to a neurologist. His diagnosis was that I had a vertebrae pressing on the nerve. He said to me, "If you want, I can schedule you for surgery tomorrow. When you wake up, the pain will be gone." What I heard was hard to believe. To think that the pain was that great, but it could just instantly go away, was so hard to believe, but that's what had happened.

From that moment on, I appreciated so much more how far we have come with medical science. But most of all, I was so lucky and blessed to have gotten back my good health. I was also fortunate enough to receive a settlement for $112,000 from the insurance company. That money gave me and Marie the opportunity to spend more time in Florida with my father.

The timing couldn't have been better. That's when my father's health started failing. Marie and I would stay for months at a time, living with him in his condo. Words couldn't express the love that I had for this man. He was my greatest hero. I don't believe there was a person who ever met him who didn't fall in love with him. I only wish that I could have been half the man that my father was.

The way my father inspired me, he said that's the same way I inspired him. I motivated him like no other. He had such confidence and belief in anything I said—I'm positive of that.

On our last trip, Boosch and I went back to see him. He was having a serious operation. He had an aneurysm in his stomach. After the operation was over, it was touch-and-go in the recovery room. The doctors thought he might not make it because his heart was very weak. I remember going into the recovery room to see him. He was lying there with his eyes closed, resting. As I began to speak and he heard my voice, I felt his spirit rise. I remember saying, "Dad, you made it buddy! You're going to be all right. You know I wouldn't lie to you. You did it! You got through it."

Well! After me saying that, I could just sense the faith that he had in his recovery. I recall a few days later, as he was in a regular hospital room recovering, he said to me in a somber voice, "I don't know, Paulie. I don't know if I want to fight anymore. I'm tired."

I said to him "Dad, I love you so much, whatever you want, whatever you feel." I could see the shock on his face at how I answered him. He knew that I loved him more than life itself, and here I was telling him that my love was so great for him, I would be willing to let him go.

Boosch and I stayed with him for a couple of months after he came home from the hospital. I remember when I told him I had to get back to Jersey for a while, he wanted to know if Marie could stay. He had really gotten close to her. He really enjoyed her company. She always made him laugh, not to mention how helpful she was around the house. For that, I will forever be grateful to her. As much as Marie wanted to stay, she had to get back to check on her elderly mother.

The one thing I left out of this story about my father is my older brother, John. The love and effort that my brother put into taking care of my father is something that will forever last in my heart. A month after Boosch and I were back home, we got the call that everyone fears, the call that bears the news of the loss of a loved one. It was about 10:00 in the evening on a Thursday when my brother, John, called. He was crying as he told me, "Daddy's gone. He passed away in his sleep on the sofa."

I told him, "I'll be on the next flight down there."

Reader, I'm not going to write about how I felt at that moment or express the sadness that I had in my heart. I believe that all of you who are reading this could relate in your own way when a situation like this comes up in their life. Life is the greatest gift that there is, and then it ends—*or does it?*

I often speak of destiny throughout my writings. Yesterday, I got a phone call from my friend, Richie Cigar, and after reflecting back to the hour and a half conversation, I feel I have to stop my writing and talk about current events. How ironic that I'm doing this, because part of our conversation was him critiquing my writing. One of his negative comments was how I kept stopping from time to time to speak of current events.

Well, I know I'm spiritually motivated in my writing, and I must go with my feelings. I have to spend some time talking about Richie Cigar at this time, because *destiny* has it this way.

I spoke of Richie Cigar earlier in the book. He's the friend who had had inoperable cancer last year, and then had a complete turn-around and became cancer-free. Well, this year while I was incarcerated, the cancer came back. I learned about this two months ago when I got out on bail.

Last month, I got this strong, spiritual feeling that Richie Cigar should be involved in this book, mainly from the standpoint of critiquing it. I don't know why I felt this way, especially since he disagrees with how I'm writing this book. Even though so much of his critiquing makes sense to me, I have to do my writing how I have been spiritually motivated to do it.

I'll give you one example. Remember the story about my arrest in Huntsville, Alabama, and how I bullshitted the detectives that I was going to be on the Johnny Carson show? He said, "That shows you have no credibility. If you're showing the reader that you were bullshitting about that, why should the reader believe anything that you're saying? Why shouldn't the reader think that anything you say is bullshit?"

Although that makes sense, I can't agree with that thinking. The way that story went is the way that story had to be told. Reader, if you remember, I told you that I was telling my life story was so that *you* could make your own opinion about my credibility.

Anyway, this last call, when I heard Richie Cigar speak in the beginning of the phone conversation, I thought he seemed weak from the tone of his voice. That didn't stop him from giving his opinion, disagreeing with how I was going about writing this book. In fact, he refused to refer to my work as a book. He said, "It's a journal you're writing, not a book." He also said, "Despite me disagreeing with every part of the way you are trying to tell your story, I can't believe your incredible conviction. I've never seen anyone in my life as possessed as you. All I get out of your writing is your mother's spirit—but I believe in that, so strongly."

Little did Richie Cigar know, but that's all I needed to hear.

Before Richie Cigar hung up the phone yesterday, he said to me, "This phone conversation has inspired and rejuvenated me. Before we talked, I was tired and weak, and now, when I hang up the phone, I'm going to help my wife cook."

Only *God* knows what destiny lies with Richie Cigar's cancer, but I believe strongly in him being part of the writing of this book.

Back to my story. So now both my mom and dad have passed on. No one could have more love for their mom and dad than I have for my parents. There's a certain sadness and emptiness that lingers on, but as nature has it, we're able to adjust and go on with our lives. For the most part, nature's normal sequence is for our parents to pass on before their children.

Now, about two years after my dad's passing, I get a phone call from my ex-girlfriend, Angie, telling me that her daughter, Karla, has passed away. Oh my *God,* I loved Karla so much. I cannot put into words the sorrow I felt for Angie. Once I love someone, that love never leaves me, so when I thought of the pain that Angie was going through, the sorrow I felt was hard to bear.

Reader, if you believe in God, I guess you could say that God works in mysterious ways. I remember a nun in my eighth grade Catholic grammar school saying, "The greatest cross a parent could carry in life is the loss of a child." I believe this to be so true.

❦ *Chapter Fourteen* ❦

Now, the next ten years seemed to be the same old thing: wagering on sports and watching the games on TV. I was going from football to basketball and then to baseball, seven days a week. The only time that routine would change is when I went to the Sands casino in Atlantic City. Besides the casino, I really never went anywhere. All my time was preoccupied with gambling.

From time to time, everyone once in a while, I would stop and think. I'd say to myself, *I'm wasting my time.* There was this feeling deep down inside of me that made me feel like I had this special purpose in my life, but those feelings would be smothered by my gambling.

The story I'm about to tell has never been told to a single person. I'm putting it on paper for the first time.

It's 9:00 on Monday morning, February 21, 2011. I'm sitting at my kitchen table. I'm looking out the window, and it's snowing. It's just occurred to me that it was February of last year, 2010, when the snow was falling, that I decided to tell my story.

In April of 2008, the most incredible phenomenon occurred. It was Sunday evening at 11:00 when I got up from the sofa in my living room where I was watching TV. I was going into my bedroom to go to sleep. As I started to enter my bedroom, I saw this dark tunnel at the opposite side of the room. In this tunnel, I saw a bright, shining light and also a number of smaller shining lights. It looked to be about eight or ten smaller lights, though I didn't count them. The tunnel started from the right side of the bedroom and went the entire length of the bedroom to the left side. On the left side, that part of the tunnel led to this wide opening that looked like outer space. It was dark like the tunnel; and through the opening, I could see numerous amounts of lights. All the lights I saw were like the little lights of the stars. The only light I saw that was much larger than any of the other lights was the one I saw in the tunnel. I also saw two lights that were at the bottom of the tunnel. They were not inside the tunnel, but close to the border of the tunnel.

As I was looking at all this, I was totally shocked. I was amazed at what I was seeing, but I wasn't scared. I asked myself if I was dreaming. Then I slapped myself in the head, and when I felt the pain, I knew I was awake.

At that moment, I walked across the bedroom and took one step into the tunnel. From the large shining light, I heard my mother's voice say, *"All our spirits live on, although we are accountable for our actions on earth."* I then heard her say, *"We can influence our destinies each and every day."*

I stood there and waited to hear more, but my mother's spirit said no more. I then tried to walk to the end of the tunnel, to the opening that looked like outer space, but

213

I couldn't get in. All I could see from the opening was the darkness and a lot of little lights. After I tried a couple of times to walk into that opening, everything disappeared. I found myself just standing there at the end of my bedroom. Then I hit myself again to make sure I was awake and not dreaming. I knew I wasn't hallucinating and I wasn't on any kind of drugs.

Believe it or not, I was in the hallway of the *Beyond the Beyond*.

I also had gotten the insight and awareness that because I tried to walk into the opening at the end of the tunnel that appeared to look like outer space, and I was unable to enter because my spirit was still living within my body. The insight that I was given is that from time to time a spirit leaves the Beyond the Beyond to go into this tunnel to visited a spirit that is still living within a body. Although I witnessed this special occurrence my insight has told me that I was unable to enter the opening to the Beyond the Beyond because this should remain a mystery to all spirits that are still living within a living body.

Reader, I bring you good news, not from me but from my mother's spirit. Our living spirits inside us live on for eternity in the *Beyond the Beyond*. One day, your heart will stop beating. That will be the end of your body and your time on earth, but it will not be the end of you. Your earthly body is just a temporary residence for your spirit.

Throughout my life, I have experienced almost everything that one could possibly experience in a lifetime. Somehow, I always had this premonition that there was a reason for it to be that way, and now I understand from my journey to the *Beyond the Beyond.*

Shortly after this occurrence took place, I got this strong spiritual feeling towards four people. The first two were Deepak Chopra and Dinesh D'Souza. I had seen them on the Larry King show; and as I listened to them talk, I knew that each of them had a special living spirit within them. As I listened to them talk, I had gotten this strong spiritual feeling that their God-given intellects had brought them to the border of the *Beyond the Beyond.* I believe that the two lights that I witnessed on the border of the tunnel were Deepak Chopra's and Dinesh D'Souza's living spirits.

The other two people that I had felt spiritually connected to were Oprah Winfrey and Don Imus. I had no idea whatsoever why I felt that way about them. Every once in a while, I would watch Oprah on TV and listen to Imus on the radio, but I knew nothing about either one of them. All I knew was that they each had a special living spirit inside. It was only last year when I got the courage to decide to write the story of the *Beyond the Beyond* that I found out that they were two of the most powerful means to spread the good news of the mystery of death.

After I came to that special conclusion, I felt I couldn't tell anyone. I questioned why this would've happened to me. People would think I'm nuts to tell this story. Even though I knew this incredible experience happened to me, and that I had so many other stories of my mother's spirit talking to me and the many signs that her spirit had given me, my common sense told me not to tell anyone.

Then, one day last year, as destiny would have it, my mother's spirit inspired me to have the courage to tell the story of the *Beyond the Beyond*. I come across a book written by Dinesh D'Souza. The name of the book is *Life After Death: The Evidence*. I recommend that anyone who doubts my story that there is life after death to our spirit should read this book.

I believe that it was destiny that this book was written, both from a scientific standpoint and also from a religious standpoint. *Life After Death: The Evidence* presents a reasoned, scientifically based case that life after death is more than possible—it is highly probable. Indeed, it has far more evidence on its side than atheistic arguments about death being our complete and utter extinction.

I also feel extremely spiritually connected to Dinesh D'Souza because of his work in the writing of his book *Life After Death*. This book tells of all the different branches of science and both sides of the debate over life after death. He's debated with all the top intellectual atheists of the world. I believe that any doubters of my message will be believers after reading D'Souza's book.

I bring the world the good news that there is life after death. I make my claim from the miracle of the *Beyond the Beyond*.

By the way, I didn't read his book, but listened to it on tape. I don't want you to think I lied to you when I said that I've never read a book.

I would like to go back to my experience in the tunnel. I had this strong insight and awareness that the other smaller lights that were in the tunnel were other people's spirits. I believe those spirits had come out of the outer space opening and into the tunnel for the purpose of reaching out to other living spirits. I also had sensed the power of my mother's spirit was so much stronger.

I also had gotten the insight and awareness that because I tried to walk into the opening at the end of the tunnel that appeared to look like outer space, I was unable to enter because my spirit was still living within my body. The insight that I was given, is that from time to time a spirit leaves the Beyond the Beyond to go into this tunnel to visit a spirit that is still living within a body. Although I witnessed this special occurrence, my insight told me that I was unable to enter the opening to the Beyond the Beyond because this should remain a mystery to all spirit's that are still living within a living body.

I'm a Christian. I was brought up Roman Catholic. I believe in God, The Almighty. I believe in Jesus Christ and the Holy Spirit. Although I was raised to have those beliefs, as I became an adult, being raised that way wasn't good enough. I had to do my own soul-searching and investigating to draw up my own conclusions on what I truly believed. My conclusion for my personal beliefs is that Jesus Christ's teachings were greater than all others for mankind. I have two favorite sayings. One is, *"The measuring stick that you use for others will be the same measuring stick used for you,"* and the other is *"Let he who is without sin cast the first stone."*

Belief is *to believe,* and the scientific fact is that with all our worldly intelligence, we prove a point to be so. Atheists may not believe in God, but they do believe. They believe that there is no God.

The point I want to make is that every living soul has a belief. You can believe there is a Higher Power or not. You can believe there is eternal life or not. You can believe what some of our scientists say that after the physical body is gone, there is no more. You can believe in what most religions teach—that there is some form of everlasting life—or you can even believe in reincarnation. You can believe in Christianity, Judaism, Islamic, Buddhism, Hinduism, or Atheism. Whatever is your choice, it is a belief.

Now, I would like to throw out my theory to you, but before I do, I want to establish one thing. *There is life after death for our spirits.* I know I'm not delusional, I know I'm completely in touch with reality, and I know that I have common sense. I know that since my mother's passing to the other side, she has contacted me numerous times. This is not a belief; it's a fact.

Now, I would like to get back to my theory trying to use all my common sense. This is a theory I have, not a fact. My mother spoke to me on her deathbed, and said, "Paulie, love the Blessed Mother Mary and the Lord Jesus with all your heart."

My theory and belief is that because some Higher Power chose my mother's spirit to be given this special powerful energy, my common sense makes me think that her beliefs in Jesus Christ are true. I didn't need this theory for my personal belief in Jesus Christ, but it just happened this way.

I want to acknowledge that my faith is my belief—it is something I believe in—but *life after death is a fact.*

My mother's spirit brings this good news to the world. I know that most religions have always claimed this. In fact, my faith in Christianity and Christ's teachings about everlasting eternal life are something I have always believed in with my heart and soul—but it was a belief I had—not a fact.

Now, the miracle of *Beyond the Beyond* has proved to me that *it is a fact*.

I would like to go back to part of what my mother said: "… although we are accountable for our actions on earth…" My interpretation of those words substantiates what I believe most religions teach: that the way we live our lives here on earth *does* make a difference on how our spirits will live in the afterlife of eternity.

Morality: this is a special gift that we human beings have been given, along with free will. We have the option to choose the way we live our lives. The last words I heard my mother's spirit speak were, "We can influence our destinies each and every day."

I'm sure you have noticed that I have mentioned destiny throughout my writings, and now you know why. Earlier, I spent some time speaking about it. I believe my message is worth repeating being that it comes from *Beyond the Beyond*. One of the greatest gifts God has given us is the opportunity each and every day to influence our destinies. How we deal with each day, positively or negatively, will determine which road our destiny is leading us on.

I will try and use my common sense for a moment with the words "positive" and "negative." If we clash the two words together and put them in a fight, you will see that round after round, the word and meaning of *positive* will always win until it finally knocks out the word and meaning of *negative*. The message I give to you is to always be positive and have faith.

It's so important that I make this point to you. I don't pretend to be some kind of prophet or some kind of holy man, because I am *not*. Again, the purpose of telling my life story is to establish that point. It's also so important that I express my belief in my mother's spirit. My mother was a good woman, but I'm sure she was far from perfect. I don't proclaim her to have any special powers on her own. What I do know is that some Higher Power (I would like to believe it's God the Almighty) has chosen my mother's spirit to have been given this special energy, allowing her to contact me.

The Bible says to beware of false prophets or false prophesies. I come to you as a sinner and an imperfect man. I proclaim to have no powers. All I do proclaim is that there is life after death, and that I know it is a fact from my journey to the *Beyond the Beyond*. I have mentioned that I have felt some kind of special awareness from my occurrence from the *Beyond the Beyond*. This is why I would like to make reference to D'Souza's one point that he makes in his book *Life After Death, The Evidence*.

Christians rarely respond to any atheistic claims that are made on the basis of science and reason. When the atheists attack them, they say nothing. Certainly some Christian groups react when their religious beliefs are directly assaulted, as in the case of atheist attempts to teach evolution as a refutation of divine creation, but even here, there is a tendency to dismiss reason and science. This makes the Christians seem parochial and anti-intellectual. As an atheist friend of mine quips, "How can these Christians be against logic and inventions?"

Actually, Christians aren't opposed to either. Rather, they recognize that to a large degree, science and reason have become enemy-occupied territories. Science and reason have been hijacked by the bad guys. And with the collaboration of many scholars, the bad guys are using science and reason in order to narrow the scope of reality— to say that "science proves this" and "reason forces us to accept that." Christians believe that reality is much bigger, and that there are ways of apprehending reality beyond rational syllogisms and scientific experiments. What looks like anti-intellectualism on the part of Christians is actually a protest against reductive materialism's truncated view of reality.

The danger of abandoning the ground of science and reason, however, is that it compels Christians to live in the land of two truths. There is one truth that we hear in church and there is another truth that we hear about in the general culture. Revelation-the language of religious faith-becomes divorced from reason, which is the language of education, work, and secular society. This produces a kind of schizophrenia, especially among Christian students and Christians who work in science and technology. Your work is based on science and your faith is based on ignoring science; the two approaches seem contradictory. Or you have the awkward dilemma of trusting either your pastor or your professors; one tells you about Scripture and the other tells you about scholarship, and there is no way to believe both.

This is a frustrating way to live, and it's an even more frustrating way to try to communicate Christian beliefs to others. After all, we live today in a secular culture where Christian assumptions are no longer taken for granted. There are many people who practice other religions, and some who practice no religion at all. The Bible is an excellent source of authority when you are talking to Christians, but it is not likely to persuade non-Christians, lapsed Christians, or atheists. In a secular culture the only arguments that are likely to work are secular arguments, and these can only be made on the basis of science and reason. Moreover, science and reason are very powerful forces in education and the media, and these institutions have a huge impact on the development of our children. To relinquish science and reason is to concede precious cultural real estate to the atheists, and to risk losing our children to atheism and radical secularism. Indeed, as pollster George Barna shows, many young Christians do give up their childhood faith and become skeptics and unbelievers. In sum, a rejectionist strategy is fatal not only because it puts Christians on the defensive, but also because it plays into the hands of the atheists.

To reclaim the hijacked territory, Christians must take a fresh look at reason and science. When they do, they will see that it stunningly confirms the beliefs that they held in the first place. What was presumed on the basis of faith is now corroborated on the basis of evidence, and this is especially true of the issue of life after death. Remarkably, it is reason and science that supply new and persuasive evidence for the afterlife-evidence that wasn't there before. The supreme irony is that the strategy designed to destroy the religious point of view. Poised as he is to kick the Christian's rear end, the atheist ends up kicking himself in the butt!

I do not have the intellect to put into words what D'Souza so eloquently does in his argument of life after death. I believe that it was destiny that his book crossed my path to help give me the encouragement to tell my story of the *Beyond the Beyond*.

The message that you should have received from my journey to *Beyond the Beyond* is that each day, we should be aware that we are accountable for our actions; and every day, we should be motivated and inspired, knowing that by living good, moral lives, we will have a reward in the *Beyond the Beyond*. The second message that we must be aware of each and every day is that we can influence our destinies by being positive, and by always making an effort to influence on what road we want our destinies to be on. If you adhere to these messages I give to you, I will guarantee you happiness in this life and your spirit's afterlife. These are not my words, but come from the *Beyond the Beyond*.

I have completed my story of occurrences that took place in my life. I have put on paper the messages I have received from *Beyond the Beyond*.

I called my pastor. I wanted him to read my manuscript and to let me know if he thought I was nuts. When I got him on the phone, he said, "You can come over right now. I have some time." So I jumped in my car and was there in five minutes, since I live only a few blocks from the rectory.

When I went into his office, I introduced myself to him, even though I've been going to his church every Sunday for the past couple of years. I have never taken the time to talk to him after church services. I told him that I've been spiritually motivated to write a book about some special occurrences in my life. I apologized to him in advance for some of the off-colored language I use from time to time, but told him that it was important for me to do it that way. I told him that the reader has to know who the true person is that is doing the writing. I let him know that although I curse, I always have respect for the person I am talking to. For example, I would never disrespect a priest, minister, or rabbi by saying a curse word in front of him. I would never curse in front of a lady or children. But the bottom line is that I do curse and use profanity.

Father Jim told me he would read my manuscript and get back to me. After two weeks went by and I did not hear from him, I was disappointed. Then that Sunday, when I was at Mass and he was giving his sermon, I felt as if he was talking directly to me and not to the congregation. He was saying that sometimes we use God for our own gratification. He was saying that sometimes we may use God for our own ego and for our own recognition and popularity. Sometimes, we may do something for our own glorification. I believe that everything he was saying was directly being said to me.

When I went home after 12:00 mass, I was totally blown out. The guilt that I had was unbearable. The anguish that I felt I had never experienced before. The thought of trying to deceive or use God made me start to throw up. As I was going over my conscience, I was losing my mind. I was debating about taking my manuscript and throwing it in the garbage, despite the year of hard work I put into it.

After being home for about an hour after Sunday mass, as I was soul-searching and seeing that what the priest said, I felt guilty. I was getting some kind of glorification to myself that I was writing a book. I was guilty of having an ego when I was writing about certain stories like winning the boxing championship, or how I started a successful business with no money, and how I found it gratifying to tell about my business ideas. As I did my soul-searching, I said, "*I am* guilty; *I did get a feeling of euphoria from telling those stories."*

As I was in turmoil over those thoughts, the phone rang. I said to myself, *"Please, let it be Richie Cigar."* As destiny has it, it was Richie Cigar on the phone. I answered the phone and I started to cry as I said to him, "I thank God it's you. I'm ready to lose my mind." I told him what message I got from the priest's sermon at Mass and that I was guilty of self-gratification in my writings.

He tried to defend me and give me comfort on my sincerity, but I told him, "I can't fool God. Only He knows what is truly in my heart and in my mind. And as I answer to Him, He knows that I am guilty of getting some self-gratification from writing my manuscript."

Richie Cigar couldn't believe how shaken I was over this. Between the two of us, we came to the conclusion that I should put the manuscript away for a week and pray that God would give me some sign if I should pursue trying to get my manuscript published.

Later that night, I went over what had happened that day with my girlfriend, Marie. She couldn't believe how affected I had become over the occurrences that happened that day. She agreed that I should take a step back and put my manuscript on the shelf for a week. So I did, and each and every day, I kept seeing signs for the entire week that told me that my story of *Beyond the Beyond* should be told.

I believe that it was destiny for that priest to have given me that message from the pulpit. The message I received is that I could never drop my guard and look for self-gratification from my story. All credit, glorification, and acknowledgment must go, at all times, to God the Almighty. My conclusion from the sermon that I believe was directed at me is that only God knows what is in my heart and mind, and we can't fool Him.

I have spoken of destiny throughout my writings. I believe with every fiber of my being that it was destiny to write this manuscript. Now we will see if a man who has never read a book and has no literary talent or skills is destined to have his manuscript published for the world to benefit from. If you, the reader, are reading this in a book form, then you will know that my destiny has been fulfilled.

When I was sixteen years old, I remember these words coming to me, and I was so very spiritually moved: "Words are impressive, but actions are convincing." Throughout my lifetime, from time to time, I felt those words had a special purpose to me. Now, in the twilight of my life, I have found the purpose of those words. I must spend the rest of my lifetime putting my words into action by spreading the good news that there is life after death.

I complete my writing on February 28, 2011, the anniversary of my mother's living spirit leaving this world for her journey to the *Beyond the Beyond*. And now you, the reader, will make the final judgment on if this book is a novel, a mystery, or an autobiography.

I thought my story was finished and the book was completed, but how destiny has it, that is not so. It took so many miraculous occurrences for my story to become a book, so I will tell the last final one. When I completed my writing I said to myself *"Now, how do I get my manuscript published? I have no knowledge of the business world of publishing."* All I knew is that it is destiny for my manuscript to become a book for my story to be told. I came up with the answer that I would use my common sense to make this happen. So I went to a Barnes & Noble book store with my girlfriend Marie and we went to the front part of many books and wrote the publisher names down. I then sent them a short summary of my manuscript, which I later found out is referred to as a query. The way it turned out was that no publishing company would even consider looking at my work without a literary agent. Of course I didn't have a literary agent, and I was told it was very hard to get one, especially if you have no experience as a writer.

Then one day, I find this little piece of paper with the name Brighton Publishing Company on it. My girlfriend Marie and I had gotten that name a week earlier at Barnes and Noble, but I had misplaced it. How destiny would have it, a week later I find it and decide to send a query to the Brighton Publishing despite knowing the odds were slim that they would consider seeing my work without a literary agent.

As it turned out they were interested in looking at my manuscript. They instructed me to send the manuscript electronically, under no circumstances would they accepted a paper manuscript, as it would automatically be sent back.

As excited as I was to hear the news that a publishing company wanted to see my manuscript, I had strong feelings not to send it electronically, but to send them the paper manuscript instead. I wanted them to physically have the manuscript in their hands.

Marie argued and fought with me not to do it that way, but I told her that's how I felt I had to do it, that it was my destiny. The way it turned out was the regular mail carrier who delivers to Brighton Publishing knew they didn't accept paper manuscripts and if they received a large parcel titled manuscript or submission, he would simply return it to the sender without delivering it. The day the manuscript arrived, the regular mail carrier was on a day off and another mail carrier was working. Not knowing their policy regarding paper manuscripts and the fact that the manuscript was too large to fit into the mail box, he went to their office to personally deliver the mail. Because Brighton Publishing has multiple adjoining suites in their office complex, there are multiple doors. The front door is unlocked and the other doors are locked. Had the mail carrier used the front door, the door announcer would have sounded and whoever was available would have gone into the lobby to see who was there and would have refused delivery of the paper manuscript. The mail carrier for some reason bypassed the front door and went to another door that leads to the publisher's office. Instead of being locked as usual, he found it unlocked. He walked in and laid the mail on a desk as the publisher was engaged in a telephone call. After the call the publisher realized the mail contained a paper manuscript submission which would have been rejected had the publisher not been on the phone. The paper manuscript ultimately found its way to the desk of acquisitions editor, Don McGuire.

Don told me he was surprised there was a paper manuscript on his desk for review. Nevertheless, he started to read it, and said once he started, he couldn't put it down. When he called me and told me that Brighton had an interest in publishing it, he mentioned he couldn't help but note the series of coincidences that occurred for him to receive the paper manuscript. I told him they were not coincidences, and that this was all part of my destiny and Brighton Publishing was destined to publish my message from Beyond the Beyond to help inspire people throughout the world.

The End

⳹ᗐ *In Gratitude* ᗐᔔ

This is an Acknowledgement to all the people who made it possible for me to obtain bail and, therefore, afford me the opportunity to be able to complete the writing of this book:

Marie Platten
Gina & Charlie King
Brian & Amy Gaccione
Marcus & Colleen Gaccione
John Gaccione
Ann Platten
Louise Lembo Kuhnle
Ron & Kim Kist
Judge Steven Barrett
Michael Torres
John & Maryann Liuzzi
Tom & Bernice Ciardella
Bob & Diane Gareffa
Rich & Carol Pezzolla
George Pepe
Babe & Maureen Ciardella
Frank Gaccione
Joe Gaccione
Rosemary & Frank Ortiz

John Gaccione, Jr.
Mark Gaccione
Donna Marie Gaccione
Joe Tondi
Tina & Dave Connelly
Joyce Luberto
Rose & Jim La Faso
Joanne Elliot Fusina
Barry Kelner
Anthony Lenza
Larry Sparta, Sr.
Rich La Manna
Mark Kesack
Ken & Diane Dovick
Marge Plucinsky
Pat Di Paolo
Joe Augnilera
Peter McEnerney

✑ About the Author ✑

A ccording to the FBI and New York's Organized Crime Task Force, Paul "Doc" Gaccione is a leading member of the Mafia. At the time of this book's release, he has been arrested and is under indictment for murder. After spending six months in Rikers Island jail, he was released on $1,000,000.00 bail.

Paul "Doc" Gaccione was born and grew up in Lyndhurst, New Jersey. An amateur boxing champion who excelled in athletics he became a leader in the physical fitness industry. He now holds a Doctorate in naturopathic medicine. He's the proud father of four children and eleven grandchildren, and his principal beliefs are is that "To demand respect, you have to give respect" and "No man should ever raise his hands to a woman."

Despite the many downfalls that occurred from time to time in his life and the many allegations against him, he has always maintained a belief in being positive. He also spends some

233

time doing motivational speaking. He presently shares his life with his girlfriend Marie.

Beyond the Beyond is his first published work, but Gaccione says, "If I become spiritually motivated to write again, I will do so."

CPSIA information can be obtained at www.ICGtesting.com
Printed in the USA
BVOW082212040112

279759BV00005B/4/P

9 781936 587520